OUT OF THE TRAP

By

Billy DeVasher

Out of the Trap

ISBN: 978-0-5781233-0-1

Copyright © 2013, Billy DeVasher
All rights reserved.

No part of this book may be reproduced, stored in a retrieval system, or transmitted in any form, or by any means, electronic, mechanical, photocopying, recording or otherwise, without prior permission of the author.

OUTLINE

Acknowledgements 5
INTRODUCTION 9
PROLOGUE 13

I.   BACK TO THE BEGINNING
    1.   The Early Years 21
    2.   Off To a Slow Start 41
    3.   Yearning for Adventure 53
    4.   The Marines or Football 67
    5.   Gung-Ho 79
    6.   Boot Camp 93
    7.   Wanderings 105

II.   FOX HILL
    8.   Fox Hill 131
    9.   Home Again 163

III.   FOR EVERYTHING A SEASON
    10.   Endings and Beginnings 171
    11.   A Season of Blessing 181
    12.   The Trap of "no education" 191
    13.   More Blessings 203

IV. SEASONS OF TRAGEDY AND TRIUMPH
14. Sweet with the Bitter 219
15. Prelude to Tragedy 233
16. Maxwell 249
17. Walking On 275

V. SEASONS OF GRACE
18. Homecoming 293
19. The Silver Star 303
20. Back to Korea 317
21. Hale and Hearty 327
22. 85 and Holding 339

EPILOGUE 353

About the Author 357

ACKNOWLEDGMENTS

ONE MORNING ABOUT a year ago when my Wife and I were having coffee, she asked me if there was anything left on my bucket list that I really wanted to do. I thought a bit and answered: "You know, I would really like to finish my book—the one I started writing twenty-two years ago and have approached with an on-and-off effort during all that time.

Soon after that, I was introduced to Joe Johnson who had been a ghost writer for 165 books which were published by the Baptist Sunday School Board and Broadman Press. We began meeting together once a week. I talked and he wrote. During the week, I would get up around three o'clock in the morning and write until I went to work. He took all of this and came up with a manuscript.

A retired book editor, who was a member of the same church that I was, agreed to read the manuscript and give his opinion. He told me: "Billy, you have a wonderful story, but you need to take a marker, go back through and mark out everything that is Joe Johnson and start all over telling it again. Tell the story yourself."

I found that difficult to do and soon became interested in another project. The book went on the shelf.

Then about 8 years after I had given my testimony to about 300 people, a gentleman, Sid Reiner, approached me: "Billy, you need to write a book. People will be blessed by reading it. I've had some experience and will be glad to help you with it."

We began meeting and he kept encouraging me to come to his house and work on the book. His help was a big factor in making progress on it, but other projects took my interest and the book landed on the shelf again.

Until a year ago when Dot, my wife, who for a time in her life was an English teacher, said, "O.K. Enough, already! We're going to see what we can do about finishing that book!" I knew that we were off and running because, in the 60 years that we've been married, she had never started a job that has not been finished."

So my sincere thanks to all of these people who have helped along the way and here it is—now it is finished!

My most important thanks goes to a Heavenly father who, for reasons I don't know, has never let me keep the story of His work in my life on the shelf!

INTRODUCTION

The question keeps running through my mind: Why would I think I could—or should—ever write a book?

HERE I AM! Well into my eighties—an octogenarian, no less. An ordinary guy who grew up in the typical American town—

- where everybody knew everybody else, and everybody else's business as well,
- where God, flag, family and apple pie were the order of the day, and were honored, revered, and cherished,
- where a handshake was all that was needed to seal a deal.

AND HERE I AM! An ordinary guy doing an extraordinary thing—who can't shake the feeling that he has lived something worth telling—a story that should be told:

- a story that just might help someone else along the way,
- or at least, be of encouragement to some who are still in the middle of the journey,
- or of interest,
- or something that will be a way of expressing my thanks to a Heavenly Father who obviously has had His hand on my life from the beginning and who has showered me with His grace and blessings—and yes, His chastening as I needed it!

Of course, we know that everybody has a story to be told. God has planned it that way—for each person is unique—different—one of a kind—and each story unique and tailored to fit the individual person.

We all have been gifted by our Creator with a special makeup, a different DNA. We are each an original, like nobody else—different fingerprints, different talents, different looks. We each have different paths to travel in this life—individual choices to make along the way.

My years have been marked with unusual blessings, but also struggles, circumstances—traps that could have made life turn out very differently were it not for the fact that the way was made for me to escape those traps—and move toward freedom! I believe that it was the hand of God moving through His gift of His Son, Jesus, who led me all the way!

This—then—is MY story!

"He ransomed me unharmed from the battle raged against me; even though many opposed me."

Psalm 55: 18

PROLOGUE

NOVEMBER 28, 1950, was very, very cold in North Korea—with temperatures ranging from 40 to 50 degrees below zero and biting winds blowing from the north. I was one of the 236 men who made up Fox Company, 7th Marines, First Marine Division, United States Marine Corps. We had been in Korea since August when we came ashore in the Inchon Landing and successfully fought our way north to liberate Seoul, Korea's capital city from the North Korean People's Army. From there, we had pushed the Communists back beyond the 38th Parallel, miles into North Korean territory and were headed for the Yalu River, which separates North Korea from Manchuria in China. A job well done, according to

General Douglas McArthur. He also said that when we reached the Yalu River, we would board a ship and be home for Christmas.

Night came, and about 11:00 o'clock we were high on Fox Hill at the Chosin Reservoir. Time to dig in and get a little rest. Normally, digging in is what we would do, but that didn't seem to be much of a priority—for we were on our way home—just a few miles from the Yalu River. Besides, the ground was frozen solid—and the temperature was 40 to 50 degrees below zero. Most of us partially dug in, eager to get some rest. It had been a long, busy day!

I did take time to set up my 30 caliber water-cooled machine gun which weighed about forty pounds and which I carried wherever I went.

Because it wouldn't be long until morning and because we were exhausted from the long day's trip up the mountain, a couple of hours rest in the sleeping bags seemed more inviting. After all, we were almost on our way home.

Suddenly about 2:00 o'clock we were wakened by the noise of bugles sounding and whistles blowing—something we'd never heard from the North Koreans before.

Then all Hell broke loose!

Enemy soldiers were coming in a steady stream up the ravine—hundreds of them! Shots were being fired. Mortars were being dropped on the hill. The noise of battle was all around us. Marines were being hit and some started calling out, "Corpsman, I'm hit."

I was out of that sleeping bag in a hurry—manning my machine gun.

We were under attack! We had no idea who the enemy was—we thought North Korean. Soon we would find that 100,000 Chinese Communist soldiers had slipped over the Manchurian Border, crossed the

Yalu River and surrounded us. They were coming at us from all sides! We were trapped! There was no way out!!

We wouldn't be going anywhere that day. Our Company, Fox Company, was surrounded, cut off from the main body of Marines, with no hope of escape from this frozen mountain called Fox Hill! And there were thousands of enemy soldiers out there with one goal in mind—kill us all! We immediately knew that the chances of our getting out of this trap alive were slim to none. We would have to fight against incredible odds to survive. No other Marines could get to us; we could not get to them. We were cut off—separated from our main body! We were hopelessly trapped…

I.

BACK TO THE BEGINNING

AT DAWN, THERE was a break in the fighting—a break in which there were no bullets flying, no enemy coming over the Pass—a break in which my mind raced to access the situation, to ask: What's going on here? Why am I here on this cold mountain in a foreign country, being shot at by people I don't know and have no ill feelings toward? What brought me here?

Immediately, a fleeting panorama began to cross my mind—a panorama of the events that had led me to this trap on Fox Hill—a situation which very well might claim my life!!

"For I know the plans I have for you," declares the Lord, "Plans to prosper you and not to harm you, plans to give you a hope and a future."

Jeremiah 29: 11 NIV

CHAPTER 1

THE EARLY YEARS

IT ALL BEGAN for me on a cold winter morning, January 18, 1928. I was born at home—as most babies were then. Home was on North Water Street in Gallatin, Tennessee, a little town located about an hour's drive from Nashville. My parents were Gene and Annie DeVasher. I was the second of three sons. My brother, David, was a year and a half older than I and Joe, a year and a half younger.

Weighing in just 2 ounces short of twelve pounds, I was ready to meet my world head-on.

My parents were hard-working, God-loving people who had the dreams and desires of most parents—to provide a better life for their children than they had. Caring for a growing family and keeping their heads above water was a struggle—for several reasons.

The first was that this was the Pre-depression era. In another year, the bottom would fall out of the economy, money would be scarce and jobs difficult to get and keep. One of my earliest memories is of my Dad coming home and telling my Mother that he and a lot of his fellow workers had been laid off. He had been working for the Louisville and Nashville railroad as a fireman. Several times I heard him tell others how he shoveled coal into the engine of the train all the way from Nashville to Louisville, having to shovel faster when the train approached a hill in order for the train to get over the hill. It was extremely hard physical work, but it was a job that provided for his family, and on this particular day that job was gone.

There were no unemployment benefits or food stamps. How was he supposed to support his family? It was a sad, sad day in the DeVasher family, one that even a four-year-old could recognize as disaster for us.

The second reason was that my Mother was a stay-at-home Mom (a fact that I came to appreciate along the way, especially when I'd come home from school in the afternoon and find a plate of homemade oatmeal cookies waiting, fresh from the oven). The problem was that meant only one income. Now there would be no income with no job for Dad.

The most significant reason though, was that my Father was a disabled American veteran, because of being gassed at the Battle of Argonne Forest during World War I. He lived with damaged lungs and kidneys. However, this didn't keep him from working as hard as he could. He was tough, but it meant he was in and out of the hospital a lot. I remember several trips I made with my Mother to visit him at St. Thomas hospital in Nashville. We caught the train early in the morning in Gallatin, left Union Station by trolley to go to the hospital where I would play around on the steps that led up to the hospital entrance and wait for my Mother to come back for me. I had never seen any building as big as this one. It was cold and uninviting. I thought I never wanted to find myself in a place like this. However, I heard my Mother talking to people about how well they took care of my Daddy, and if they helped him get well, the place was all right with me.

Somehow, in spite of the insecurity that must have pervaded their lives, my parents managed to provide us with the love, attention, and yes, discipline that we needed to enjoy a fairly normal childhood and become productive adults.

EARLY IN MY life, I was introduced to the in's and out's of capitalism. The name of the game was to find something you could do that somebody else needed done. Do it well and there would be a reward coming—that reward would hopefully be monetary.

My brother, Dave, and I began by working a paper route. Somewhere along the way, I accumulated enough money to buy a used bicycle, which cost seventy-five cents—and I made a deal to pay for the bicycle on the installment plan with no interest to be paid! Seemed like a good idea to me!

The bicycle meant I had wheels and the opportunities to find odd jobs. Some I found were helping in the tobacco field or the watermelon patch where the greatest reward was sometimes a home cooked meal with the boss' family—plus fifty cents a day! Maybe!

One of the best jobs I had was loading watermelons from the field onto a wagon pulled by mules and going to town where I could help sell them. My job was to deliver the watermelons from the wagon to the porches of the families who bought them. The kids were always really glad to see the watermelons coming.

Two things were engrained early in me. One was the pleasure that came with working hard and receiving the reward that results from that, and two, the satisfaction of having a relationship with people, especially when you are helping them. Both of these discoveries were to influence my life in positive ways as I grew up.

IT SOON BECAME obvious to my parents that raising three strong, energetic, creative boys was a daunting endeavor! With careful consideration, they got the idea that the solution to the problem was to buy a farm. It seemed to be a good idea—to harness all that energy and in the process help contribute to the making of a living, grow our own food, and keep those three young men so busy they wouldn't have time to get into trouble.

So, when I was eleven years old, my family moved to a small farm on the outskirts of Portland, Tennessee. A farm! With animals that had to be tended to, pigs that had to be fed, hay that had to be sowed, harvested, baled, and loaded into trucks for selling, twelve to fifteen cows that had to be milked —twice a day—on and on it went! We would get up before dawn, milk the cows, strain the milk, pour the milk into large cans, get the cans to the road to be picked up by the Kraft Milk Company, and try to be dressed and ready to board the school bus on time. If we didn't make it on time, it meant walking (or running) to school! But living on a farm with all that was involved certainly solved the problem for our parents. We were pretty well exhausted after the day's activities—which always included practice for one of the sports—football, basketball, or baseball.

MOVING TO A new town meant enrolling in a new school. Mother took us there. I was dressed in my best clothes—knickers! Knickers were the hot item in Gallatin! High fashion! But that wave of fashion had not yet hit Portland! It didn't take too many sidelong glances and snickers about the knickers for me to confine the knickers to the back side of the closet and turn to overalls! Soon all was well!

OUR LIVES WERE simple and uncluttered. We couldn't afford clutter anyhow. We worked without complaint to do our part to keep the family afloat. We attended school and church. Going to church was second nature to us. I would even walk several miles to church by myself when my family didn't go. Being in Church has always had a special appeal to me—even though at times that appeal was purely social. And on Easter Sunday when I was thirteen years old, my brother and I became members of the Methodist Church in our town.

Later, when we were still teenagers, that Church grew and needed to build a new building, My Dad, Dave, and I had the pleasure of moving an old rock fence, rock by rock, lifting each stone onto our Dad's old truck and taking each one to the site of the new Methodist Church It seemed to me that we were doing something really, really important—maybe like building a cathedral where the Lord Himself would be honored and worshipped for years and generations to come. That experience made a lasting impression on my life. I still look at it as one of the highlights of anything I have accomplished in my life.

WE HAD NEVER heard the word, "dysfunctional", as related to a family—and wouldn't have known what it meant if we had. We lived together as a family with the normal number of complaints and happy times—ups and downs and fights between Dave and Joe and me. (We hadn't heard of sibling rivalry either.) I still carry the scars of one of those when my younger brother, Joe, and I were having a disagreement and he pulled a knife on me and cut my thumb almost off. I wrapped a towel around my profusely bleeding hand and ran the two miles to the doctor's office to get stitches by myself that day. After that, Joe and I found other ways to settle our differences. My Mother said that fights with Dave came to an end the day that I came out on top and whipped him good. Dave had not realized that I had grown larger and stronger than he and somehow, (my Mother said) he lost his desire to fight with his younger brother after that encounter.

WITH ONLY ONE car in the family—and 3 boys—each one beginning to want to take his favorite girl (at the moment) out, it was probably amazing that there wasn't a whole lot more conflict and competition between us, but the truth was that we actually loved each other and maintained a mutual respect and admiration for each other throughout our lives.

MENTIONING THE CAR reminds me of the day I swapped my jersey calf for a car.

My Dad was a horse and mule trader. He also bought and and sold cows and calves. One day a man came by looking at cows and saw a calf he really liked. It was my jersey calf, my show calf. I took a class in agriculture in my freshman year of high school. Every student had to have a project for the class. My project was this beautiful jersey show calf. My agriculture teacher had come to the farm to check it out and had approved my raising it as an acceptable project for me.

Every football player took his class. It was an easy subject and a passing grade—for sure. Everybody passed Mr. Bryant's class. Two of the best players on the team, Bob and Tony needed an extra credit but they had a problem. They lived in town, not on a farm. Mr. Bryant told them they had to have an agricultural related project to qualify for the class.

So Bob and Tony each got a chicken and kept it in their back yard. It worked. They passed the class.

Back to my jersey calf. The gentleman wanted to buy the calf but told my Dad he was short on cash. He did, however, have a car he was willing to trade for the calf. Dad told him the calf belonged to me and I was called to join the conversation. What did I think about trading the calf for the car? The idea was big time to me. "Sure, let's trade." I was fourteen years old and hated to see the calf go but it was nice to have the car. It quickly became the family car.

LOOKING BACK TO those years, I realize two things: life was tough. Winters were cold and summers were hot—no air conditioning and only grates with small fires for heat—no indoor plumbing, therefore no running water and no bathrooms. We sometimes had to break the ice on the bucket that hung outside the back door to get a drink of water.

I also know that life during my growing up years in Portland was pretty good. There were a lot of friends, plenty to do for fun, teachers who cared for you, a church where people loved and respected each other and where God was worshipped with reverence and awe! Having a personal relationship with Jesus was not yet a concept in my life. This was to come later in a vivid experience!

And there was always plenty to eat. Everybody had plenty to eat, mostly because they grew their own food. Our garden would have made Better Homes and Gardens magazine proud! Thanks to my Mom! We ate amazingly well: fruit and vegetables fresh from that garden, meat and milk from our cows and country ham, sausage, and bacon from our hogs, thanks to the annual hog killing when the first frost came in the fall! There was also the community Beef Club where 12 or 13 farm families would join together and share their beef. It worked this way. For 12 or 13 weeks one family would provide a calf — about 300 lbs. of meat—which would be shared for that weekend by the other families. That made for plenty of good beef for the fall months.

THERE WERE REASONS that our family maintained a reasonable amount of harmony. Our upbringing, the expectations of our parents and grandparents, Christian teachers and teachings, and the reality that we had so little free time. We were dead tired from working, going to school, practicing and playing sports. There was no time for anything else. "Idle hands are the devil's workshop" was an oft-repeated phrase (and belief) around our house.

There were so few problems and people getting into trouble that our town had only one policeman—and he didn't have a car!

As with everybody, I treasure memories from those growing up years—memories of delivering newspapers on my bargain bike, handing out movie announcements for the Roxy Theater and receiving free tickets as pay, emptying the pool hall spittoons in exchange for a free game, setting up pins in the bowling alley, laboring in the tobacco field and on the watermelon wagon, going door to door as an iceman delivering large chunks of ice for people's iceboxes, going hunting with my Dad on

Thanksgiving Day. He was the best hunter around. Quail season started on that day so we had an abundance of fresh quail which Mom knew how to fry perfectly. Later on, there was always a football game. Even now, Thanksgiving is my favorite holiday.

I liked to hunt in those days. It was an activity I usually shared with my Dad. My memories of hunting include my experience with box rabbit traps. These were boxes about the size of a shoebox. I'd put an apple in the back part of it and attach a string to the door. When the rabbit came to get the apple, it would trigger the string and the door would close. It was always a big thrill to bring a rabbit home because my mother knew just how to barbecue them and we would have a great supper that night.

IN RETROSPECT I realize we were exceedingly rich. We had little money but great wealth that money cannot possibly buy: family love, mutual respect, shared responsibility, the loving care of an at- home mother, the encouragement and support of a father who stood with us and stayed with us, and a deep and unshakeable belief in a Heavenly Father who loved us and sought and welcomed our worship of Him.

However, as most teenagers, I was yearning to grow up. I think there's a strong possibility that this created in me an unrest, a deep desire for more. I never complained about our chores or school, but often I found myself fantasizing about "faraway places with strange sounding names." I often didn't feel like doing the chores. Sometimes it was too hot and at others too cold, but I had my work cut out for me. I knew I was making my contribution to life and I did my work, But deep inside me, there was this yearning to see what was going on in the world out there—and especially to be one of those guys going off to fight on distant battlefields.

Soon my ever-present dream came to be one of becoming a United States Marine fighting in the Pacific.

"Are not five sparrows sold for two copper coins and not one of them is forgotten by God. But the very hairs of your head are all numbered. Do not fear, then, you are of more value than many sparrows!"

Luke 12: 6-7 nkjv

CHAPTER 2

OFF TO A SLOW START

STARTING SCHOOL was a thrill for me. I especially loved lunch—and recess, of course—but lunch was particularly special. We brought it from home and Mom would often put pieces of homemade cake in there for us. She was a master at making cakes—from scratch. They were so good that the word got around about how good they were. So I often was known to sell my cake instead of eating it—if the price was right, that is!

School itself, however, was a puzzle for me from the beginning. I loved going there to be with the other kids, but dealing with the work had no interest for me. It was a challenge I didn't want to tackle. Maybe the fact that I had both the mumps and measles that first year of school and missed some valuable fundamental stuff had a crippling effect for me. Maybe it didn't help any that I was always fascinated with the people around me and what was going on with them—and didn't pay much attention to the main one—the teacher. Whatever it was, I got off to a bad start and failed the first grade. That put me a year behind and meant I had a problem with the basics of reading. It was too much trouble to try to figure it all out. So I didn't—and I failed first grade. I was a failure before I even got out of the starting gate!

I have met very few people who have failed first grade. In my years in education I haven't been able to figure out how that happened.. I remember experiencing a lot of hurt in becoming aware that I was a failure—I know now that failing that grade didn't make me a failure, but I certainly felt like one.

The memory of returning to school that next year and being in the first grade again is very real to me. These were the days before air conditioning and the windows were open.

I saw my friends from the year before in a second grade line passing by and I wondered why I wasn't good enough to be with them. They had moved on and here I was—stuck in first grade. There must be something wrong with me, I figured.

Those few of us who have failed first grade know it is a big deal. You are face to face with failure but you're not old enough—or wise enough—to know how to deal with it. You don't even know why you failed. You thought you were doing what everybody else was doing. Then you're told something is wrong with you. You're stuck here and everybody else—all your friends—are going ahead to a good place. You are stuck! You're trapped! You're hurt! Hurt in a place where it brought tears. Everyone else was one of the good people. I was bad! I thought I was as smart as all the other kids—a winner in my own eyes! But now I am a loser!

A sad comment—I didn't learn to read much better the second time around. In fact, I didn't learn to read very well until many years later. I found myself caught in another trap, severely handicapped in the area of education. It was many years later that I was freed from that trap.

I struggled through until the eighth grade when it was becoming increasingly obvious that I might not move over to the high school building with my classmates. One day near the end of the year, my teacher, "Miss Mamie", called me aside and said, "Billy, you know you're not doing well in your studies. You're way behind. Yet, you're so big for your age that I'm going to pass you to the ninth grade, even though you don't deserve it. You're looking like a grown man, and we're at war with Japan and Germany, and pretty soon our country is going to be needing you to help fight the war." She didn't know it but the thought of being in the military, especially the Marine Corps, made me have goose bumps—Happy goose bumps!

To this day, I've always been grateful to Miss Mamie for passing me on to the 9th grade so I could go with my classmates to the high school building across the circle that next year. The high school building was separated from the elementary school by a circle drive. Taking the trip across that circle was a step everybody looked forward to, a big deal it was when you made the move to the other side of the circle, a real milestone!

Though she's been gone many years, I would like to be able to assure her that she did the right thing in passing me on, because I eventually turned my circumstances around—got out of the trap of being educationally handicapped and went on to earn a college degree plus three graduate degrees.

But more about that later!

PARADISE FOR ME when I was around eleven or twelve was visiting our relatives in the far-off city of Louisville, Kentucky. My Grandfather, Grandmother, and many aunts, uncles, and cousins lived there. I considered them our rich kin folks. They weren't, of course. Rich, that is. They were just hard working folks who lived comfortably, and living 170 miles from my house, they seemed to have fascinating lives. The trips to see them was the fartherest I'd ever been away from home. The train trip, by myself, staying for a week were exciting. My Uncle Bob met me at the train station and another relative would take me back when the week was over. It was an adventurous experience for me.

They lived in a blue collar neighborhood. There was no crime or violence. They didn't even lock their front doors. In the evenings, in summer time, families would sit on their front porches—no air conditioning—(it was cooler out there than it was inside) relaxing and waiting until the house got cool enough to go to bed. Some would cool down by going to the neighborhood "beer garden", a neighborhood restaurant down on the corner which had a small garden with tables inside the picket fence.

The families who wanted to just sit on their porches would often send someone down there with a galvanized bucket and get it filled with beer. nobody got drunk. Nobody caused a disturbance. The adults relaxed and talked and told jokes or stories and laughed and brought a pleasant end to the day.

What an exciting week for me!

One quite memorable trip was in 1937 when the Mississippi River overran its banks and flooded stores, businesses, and homes in the downtown area. My uncle took me on a tour to see firsthand what was going on. I had never seen anything like that before and have never forgotten the scenes I saw. Those images are still in my mind and will be there for a long time.

OTHER IMAGES STAY with you—such as the day my Dad was laid off from his railroad job which I've mentioned before. It would have been much worse had it not been for a good friend of his who was the sheriff of Sumner County. He needed another deputy and my Dad needed a job. Seems the Lord is good at taking care of people's needs!

Our whole family used to go to the sheriff's office in Gallatin on Saturday night. We'd park on the square. Other friends and family would meet us there and we kids would eat Moon Pies and drink soda while the grown-ups visited with each other—and gossip until time to go home to bed. That was our social life—going to town on this one night of the week—not to carouse or "party", but to have fun and fellowship with friends, relatives, and neighbors. This was a welcome respite from the work of the week and a joyful prelude to Sunday morning when we were usually always in the place of worship.

AS A DEPUTY sheriff, one of Dad's main responsibilities was chasing down bootleggers. He worked with a group called the Revenuers. Their job was to locate people who were involved in making illegal moonshine. One night while making a raid on a still, the bootlegger ran away through the woods. Dad shot in his direction to get him to stop, but unfortunately, the shot hit the man and he died. That tore my Dad up because he was not a man of violence. I can hear him tearfully telling my Mother about it. She was wiping blood off his leg where he was hurt in the chase. It was something he never got over.

A few years ago I was in that neighborhood looking at a farm to buy. I stopped at a country store and met a man there who, when he found out my name, asked, "Hey, did you know Gene DeVasher?" to which I replied, "Yes, sir, he was my father." The man launched into details about what happened in that incident. He bore down, "I want to tell you. Your Daddy somehow was protected cause there were fellows out here who would've killed him if they'd had a chance. Yes Sir, there were a bunch of mad men all around these parts."

Dad was a man who never intended harm to any single, solitary soul. He was doing his job, taking care of his family, upholding the law. He was never really well for the rest of his life and died when he was only 56 years old.

"Lean not to your own understanding. In all your ways, acknowledge Him and He will direct your path."

Proverbs 3: 5-6 nkjv

CHAPTER 3

YEARNING FOR ADVENTURE

IN THE FALL OF 1943, I was a freshman in Portland High School (at that time it was named Sumner County High). I was so happy to be there—feeling ten feet tall and trying to fit in with my older brother's crowd of friends. Soon I was an item with a senior girl. That was big stuff—going with an older woman. School wasn't very interesting—even high school—classroom and books and homework and study—boring—but life in the social world had a lot to offer, and I had a yearning for whatever it had to offer. A restlessness developed in my spirit and soon became a part of me!

I had a friend, Earl Duncan Vanatta, who shared my yen for adventure, for being where the action was. We were especially frustrated with our age—not being old enough to join the Marines—with the war being on and all—and we talked seriously about joining the Merchant Marines together because they would actually accept sixteen-year-olds upon approval of their parents. We felt sure we could get our parents' o.k. I didn't pursue that idea, however, because my compelling desire was not the Merchant Marines but THE UNITED STATES MARINES. To me being a "Leatherneck" was the genuine mark of being a man. I was not willing to settle for anything less than that. That plan—to join the Merchant Marines—went on hold, but not the dream.

There was nothing left to do but to find fun and adventure wherever we could within our limited environment.

However, some of the time what seemed to me to be fun turned out not to be fun at all! ….The fall of my sophomore year I went into "Miss Marie's" English class and headed for the back row, which was my usual position in every class—late, as usual. Three or four guys were sitting in chairs leaning back against the wall. When I went by Slug's chair (short for Slugger), I kicked the front legs of the chair out from under him and it fell—and he fell—all over the place.

Miss Marie saw what I had done and said—in her calm, but firm, way: "Billy—go to the principal's office." Words you never want to hear! I was afraid of Mr. Jett. Everybody was afraid of Mr. Jett, but there I was—me and Slug Moore.

"Why are you here?" Mr. Jett calmly asked.

"I don't know. I went by and accidentally hit his chair and he fell. He was propped back and I couldn't get by him."

Slug tuned in: "You kicked the chair—on purpose."

Slug went back to class and Mr. Jett addressed me,

"I'm going to expel you for three days, beginning now."

I had to leave school immediately. What would I do? My Dad would really come down on me. I couldn't go home. I went to the pool room, the hangout. Nobody was there. Then I walked five miles home but nobody was there, and decided to go back to school and face Mr. Jett again.

"My Dad told me I couldn't come home. I have to come back to school." Mr. Jett and my Dad were friends. "And take my punishment here."

"All right! Go to the dressing room." That meant the paddle. It burned me up. I hurt for days. I dare not tell a soul—at school—at home—anywhere!

But somebody saw Mr. Jett walk out of the dressing room with the paddle in his hands...and then saw me. I had left my books in the English class. I knew I would find Slug Moore and beat him up, but when school was out, I had cooled off and had arrived at the conclusion that I would never do anything anymore that would land me in Mr. Jett's office again!

A BETTER PART of my growing up experience involved our neighbor's dairy business. He had a barn that was beyond belief. It had concrete floors and an upscale operation for milking cows. It actually had automatic, electrified "milkers" Just attach the milker and the work was mostly done for you. All a person had to do was get the milk from the pail to the milk cooler as quickly as possible.

There were also perks to that chore! On really hot days, after we finished work, Mr. Austin would take us (my brother and me) in his pickup truck to the Sportsman Lake, a lake built by workers under the administration of President Roosevelt. It was a beautiful lake, which looked much bigger to me at the time than it really was, but big enough to provide a formidable challenge to me— for I hadn't learned to swim the first time we went. Dave and Mr. Austin started swimming into the deep part, swimming all the way across the lake. I played around in the shallow water for a while until I decided swimming didn't look too hard to do. I would try it! I would swim across the lake! By myself! And I did! I made it—by the hardest! I look back now and know it was foolish to attempt such a feat, first time out with no one around for support! But by some miracle I reached the other side! In spite of the feelings that I was going under several times. And I could now swim! What a great feeling that was!

Our trips to the lake served another purpose! We had no indoor plumbing in our house—showers were impossible. The local barber shop provided shower facilities for 25 cents—we went there occasionally, but the lake provided a refreshing way to wash away the sweat of the day!

AT THAT TIME, most of us had never heard of drugs—certainly not recreational drugs. We only knew the kind prescribed by the family doctor and we usually didn't want to take them. Drugs were referred to as "medicine", not drugs, even though the pharmacies were usually called "drug stores". The idea of "recreational" drugs had not yet surfaced, therefore, we knew nothing of the lure associated with them nor, in fact, of how hazardous they were to your health.

But there were cigarettes! And every movie and advertisement proclaimed the pleasures and sophistication associated with smoking. To be holding one in your hand with smoke curling upward to your nose was the grown-up thing to do. It would make a man out of a boy. It was the accepted thing to do. Our school principal even designated a special area out behind the school building and soon it became known as the location of "The Chesterfield Club". Those guys (no girls—nice girls didn't smoke—at least in public) who smoked could go there during breaks. I didn't join that group—but did start smoking, and soon I was caught in a trap that would hold me hostage for years, rob me of hard earned money, and cause me some difficult days in a struggle to be free. It wasn't long before I was right in the middle of "the Nicotine trap"—a trap which was to hold me prisoner for several years!

LIVING ON A farm meant there were certain times of the year when extra help was needed to plant and harvest crops at the proper times. A gravel road ran beside out farm back to a community called Old Field. This community was populated by people whose skin color was different from mine. These folks had dark skin. At that time they were called Negroes or by some the N word. Today, the politically correct term is African-Americans. Several of the men helped us on the farm regularly. Their wives usually went into town to do housework for some of the women in town.

On the night of January 21, 2013, my son was visiting with my wife and me. We were watching a ceremony on television commemorating the birthday of Dr. Martin Luther King, Jr. when Al asked me,

"Dad, how were blacks treated when you were growing up?"

My answer was hesitant. "At the time, I thought they were treated o.k., but later on, I realized they were not treated good at all.

Their pay was probably about a dollar a day and maybe lunch. When we went in to lunch—which was ample and delicious, we came out of the field laughing and talking, but we didn't sit at the same table and eat.

Their children were not permitted to attend the same school I did. Separate and unequal. They had their own school—a one room building with one teacher for first grade through eighth grade. Not much of a building—close to their church, which was called Parker's Chapel. When they finished 8th grade—with all the grades, one through eight, in the same room with only one teacher, the children had to go to the only high school in for county for them. It was located in Gallatin, some 18 miles away. For the few who went on to high school, they had to walk up a gravel road to catch the school bus and ride the 18 miles to Gallatin. It left early and got back late.

A few finished and went on to Tennessee State University, but not many. They were needed to go to work and help support the family. One of the boys from that community went to a university in the east and received a Ph.D. degree. It was a rare event—not only for the community but for the whole county.

One summer, Alf Groves worked for us. He was a big man and strong. He worked hard. I never heard him complain. I considered him a friend and didn't pay much attention to the fact that he was treated differently than the workers who were white.

Another person from that community who worked for us was Art Dye. One day I asked him about being colored. He laughed and answered me this way:

"Mr. Billy, you are the colored one. We are working out here in the sun together and you take your shirt off. You start out white. Then you turn pink and then you get brown. I'm the same color as when we started. Mr. Billy, you are the colored one." We laughed about that—and I thought about it. Maybe I am the colored one. Maybe it wasn't much of a laughing matter to Art!

I loved Art. I loved all the people with black skin who lived in Old Field. I wondered how he made it through the winters because there was little work for him, and being young and naïve, I didn't pay enough attention to the difference that was being shown to him and his.

"I am confident of this: I will see the goodness of the Lord in the land of the living. Wait for the Lord; be strong and take heart and wait for the Lord."

Psalm 27: 13-14 niv

CHAPTER 4

THE MARINES OR FOOTBALL

THE HARD WORK on the farm and the struggle to pass my school subjects was all worthwhile to me because of football. I lived for the time on the field practicing or playing the game. Football was my reason for being.

If you are a football buff, you have heard of General Robert Neyland, for years the head football coach of the University of Tennessee Volunteers. He believed in the philosophy of "three yards and a cloud of dust", a strong kicking game and practically no passing.

Nearly every high school football team in the state of Tennessee followed his prescription for playing the game "Rock 'em and sock 'em. Hit 'em hard. Run the ball right at 'em". That's what he believed and taught. It seemed to work. So that's what we did at Portland High School. The University of Tennessee was one of the last teams in the United States to convert to the T-formation, all because of Coach Neyland's influence. That's what we did at Portland High School!

Football was different from what it is now. The helmets we wore were leather, and if you wanted one, you furnished it yourself. Many of the boy's parents wouldn't let them participate in extra-curricular activities because they were needed at home to help keep the farm operating. Our parents encouraged us to play sports. After football practice, which was during school hours, we would dress, get on the bus and go home to do the work waiting for us.

Nobody had a car of his own. There was usually a family car that belonged to our parents which we could use occasionally with parents' permission. When we started dating, it became complicated with three boys—each vying for his turn at the wheels.

IT SEEMS THAT nearly everybody my age easily remembers where they were and what they were doing on that Sunday, December 7, 1941, the day the Japanese decimated our fleet at Pearl Harbor, Honolulu. Hawaii was not yet a state, just a territory but we had military bases there and many military personnel lost their lives that day.

The afternoon of December 7, 1941, my Dad and I had gone into town for a Sunday afternoon treat of ice cream at the drug store soda fountain. A radio was playing music in the background. The program was suddenly interrupted and we heard the announcer from NBC say, "The Japanese have bombed Pearl Harbor, and our nation's Pacific fleet is in ruins."

Japan was just a place in the geography book to me, and I definitely had never heard of Pearl Harbor. My father, being a decorated veteran of World War I, understood the significance of this announcement all too well. Years later I would read of my Dad's heroism at the Battle of Argonne Forest when we discovered a faded government document confirming his valor. He had never spoken of this to any of us.

When Dad explained the situation to me, that the bombing of Pearl Harbor meant our country would be at war, my whole being came alive with the expectation of what was ahead. My first reaction— "Great! I would get to fight for our country like my Dad did'. I wanted to be in on the action!

The bombing of Pearl Harbor and Congress' Declaration of War against Japan (and later, its Axis allies) changed our lives in a dramatic way. It united our nation as nothing else had ever done before. A patriotism was born such as we had not known for a long while. Care, concern for others, and a sense of national meaning and pride surfaced. Civilians, industry, and businesses all over the country seemed to come together into an army alongside the growing Armed Forces themselves. Even stay-at-home Moms began to enter the world of work. Our national defense became the most powerful offense in the history of civilization.

Every household responded to the call. Most eligible males either volunteered or were drafted to serve in the military. Each family geared up to cooperate with the rationing of items needed in the war effort. No one complained about the ration stamps that limited essential items to every person. Precious metals that were needed for weapons, airplanes, etc., were salvaged and used for making the needed equipment for the war effort. Signs of military were everywhere.

BECAUSE THE TERRAIN in middle Tennessee was similar to that of the area where some of the fighting in the war was taking place, it was selected for practice war games for the troops. In the fields, near our home, several units of soldiers engaged in training exercises, which were called maneuvers. These men were a part of General George Patton's Tank Brigade and would soon be on the front lines of the war. These guys, many of whom were away from their homes for the first time in their lives, were welcomed warmly by our community. Homes were opened to them. Town officials paid special attention to them. Churches made extra efforts to make them feel comfortable and welcome. They were treated like royalty.

A few local girls became engaged to a few soldiers. After the war, the guys returned and married the girls and raised families. One of them later became mayor of Portland.

Some of the units camped in the woods near our house. Because it was cold weather, some of the soldiers discovered our barn and would come up and sleep where there was plenty of straw or hay on which to put their sleeping bags. My Mother often fixed hot breakfasts for them. For me, it was an exciting time. Not only did I enjoy the excitement of being around these guys, but I discovered an entrepreneurial activity for myself as well.

They wanted real food instead of C rations, like hamburgers. I could get that for them without any trouble by riding my bike to the local café in town and bringing them fast food—still warm and special order. Tips were generous and welcome!

One soldier gave me a pair of boots—the kind worn in tanks. Another gave me a field jacket. Even though it was part of an Army uniform, not a Marine uniform, I thought it was very special to wear them. They were great guys. Occasionally, some of them would come to our house at night and sit around the fire and talk about their homes, what life was like where they came from, their families and girlfriends—guys from New York, Oklahoma, faraway places that I dreamed of visiting. They were interesting guys. It was an exciting—and lucrative—time for me.

My fascination with the military was increased as I watched these guys. It seemed to me as if it would be the best adventure of all to be in their shoes. Just one problem though—they were Army soldiers—not Marines. As appealing as they were, Marines would have pleased me more.

It was sobering, however, to realize that soon these young men, soldiers, would be on the front lines risking their lives to protect our country. Sobering, but exhilarating! How I wished to be old enough to sign up with the Marines. Just maybe… maybe…the war would last long enough for me to be of an age to get in on the action. It never occurred to me that most people were praying that it would not last that long!

This was living during the time period that Tom Brocaw referred to as "the greatest generation". I know how privileged I was to be a part of that generation. Never has there been a time quite like it.

Billy at 17—yearning to be a Marine

Billy at 17—playing football

"Be anxious for nothing, but in everything by prayer and supplication, with thanksgiving, let your requests be made known to God; and the peace of God, which passes all understanding will guard your hearts and minds through Christ Jesus."

Philippians 4: 6-7 niv

CHAPTER 5

GUNG-HO

TO BE A MARINE had become my insatiable desire. For three years following our Declaration of War, I kept up with war news—through radio and the newspapers—every day wishing I could instantly grow older and become a Marine. I especially focused on the Marines in the South Pacific because there were guys from Portland fighting in that area. There was a small movie theater in town and one night I went to see a movie called "Guadalcanal Diary". It was a legendary movie of how the Marines were fighting the Japanese to keep an air field open.

Many Marines were wounded or killed. They were heavily out-numbered, but they fought for days, weeks, months and finally won the victory at Guadalcanal.

That movie thrilled me and enforced my dream of becoming a Marine. I envisioned myself in combat gear, firing at the enemy, engaging in hand-to-hand combat with a bayonet. My desires intensified.

Our Marine's costly, but resounding, victory on that South Pacific Island was a morale booster for everybody. It and our Navy's smashing defeat of the Japanese Imperial Navy at Midway turned the tide in the Pacific and put our troops on the road to Tokyo. I was ready but too young. But in my heart, I was already a Marine.

In our town, people seemed to gravitate to the local drug store where they heatedly discussed the attack on Pearl Harbor, "a day that will live in infamy", and the Pacific and European campaigns of the war. I was close to fifteen years old at the time. The first Marine I had ever met attended our high school football banquet that year. He had graduated from Portland High School three years earlier when he enlisted in the Marine Corps. He had actually fought on Guadalcanal where he was wounded and sent home. How I wanted to step into his shoes and replace him on the battle field.

During his short speech at the banquet he stated that the attributes of being a winning football player were similar to those of being a successful Marine. That reinforced my belief that the day would come when I, being a better than average football player, could soon be a good Marine.

Time passed slowly—until my time finally came….

January 18, 1945—the date of my seventeenth birthday finally arrived. The night before this birthday, I slept very little because I was making my plans for the next day—a special day!. Early that morning I was out of bed early, milked the cows, ate breakfast and caught the bus to school. This morning, however, I did not go into the school building. I walked around to the back of the bus and waited until everybody else was inside. Then I left and walked to town—probably about 15 minutes—to Main Street where all the businesses were located. One of the places we hung out was at the pool hall. I stopped there briefly, debating with myself whether I should follow through with my plan or go back to school. The plan won!

I headed out to the main highway and hitchhiked to Nashville—about 50 miles away. I knew where the recruiting office was because I had been there a couple of times earlier knowing that my time would come. Soon I was standing in the United States Marine Corps recruiting office telling the sergeant that I was there to join the Marine Corps.

"Two questions," he said. "How old are you?" and "Do you have your parents' consent?"

I told him I was seventeen and yes, I did have my parents' consent—which, of course, I didn't. (I dare not mention to them what I was doing that day). They thought I was in school and that I would travel with the basketball team that night to Nashville and would be getting home late. Dad volunteered to milk the cows for me. Absolutely nobody knew that I would be joining the Marines that day—or trying to anyway.

The Recruiting Sergeant handed me some papers to fill out—which I did. He looked them over. Then he looked me over. I was a pretty good sized kid—raised on the farm, worked hard, played sports, was in good shape. So he said: "Get undressed for your physical."

A red line on the floor led from one examining station to another. I was passing each examination with flying colors… until we got to the last station ….and there in front of me was an eye examination chart to read. I read the top line and some of the second and the examiner asked: "Do you wear glasses?" My quick reply was, "No, I don't need glasses."

He hesitated and my heart stood still when he said: "Your vision is probably good enough for the Army, but it isn't for the Marine Corps. Sorry—we can't take you."

I couldn't believe what I was hearing. My heart was broken. My whole world had just fallen apart. I didn't want to be in the Army. I didn't want to be anywhere but in the Marine Corps!"

I met the basketball team bus at Eighth Avenue and went with them to play in the game that night at David Lipscomb.

I was certainly down! But not out!

A few weeks passed. The Marines were going ashore at Iwo Jima and I was desperately trying to figure out how to join them in the Pacific. One day I came up with what I thought was a brilliant idea—why hadn't I thought of this sooner? I was about to embark on another mission to accomplish my goal. I wasn't sure the plan would work, so again I couldn't mention to anyone what I was about to do.

The plan was simple. My grandparents lived in Louisville, Kentucky. When I was 13 years old, I had ridden the train up there to spend a week with them—remember? They were always glad to see me. I told my Mom I wanted to go spend a few days with them. She thought it was fine and made arrangements for me.

There was a U.S. Marine Corps recruiting officer there. I could start over in my efforts to become one of them.

The next night I was on the bus to Louisville. The trip took several hours. It was the wee hours of the morning when I arrived at the bus station there so I found an empty bench and slept until morning. I had very little money—enough for a carton of milk and a donut. I ate that, picked up my bag, walked out, located the Federal Building, and within the hour, I was again standing before an officer in the United States Marine Corps recruiting office.

He asked me where I was from and I gave him my grandparents' address—St. Louis Avenue, Louisville, Kentucky. He looked me over, asked me the same two questions I'd heard in Nashville, gave me the same enlistment papers, pointed out where my parents would sign to give their consent and directed me to the red line that would take me through the physical exam process.

At this time, the Marine Corps had lost about 6000 Marines on Iwo Jima—that many wounded or dead—and they were looking for a "few good men" to replace them. I knew within myself that I had to be one of them.

The line was long and moved slowly. I was passing every station, again with flying colors. No problems, except the ominous eye chart loomed ahead. I was about four men back. What to do? I began to get really nervous—and then scared. How could I have been so confident that I could pass this exam? I must have been out of my head.

Just as I stepped up to try to read the chart, the recruiting Sergeant stepped in front of me—and I thought: "Now I've had it; they already know about me." He held up a pouch with half dollar coins in it and pointed the group to a nearby restaurant where it was possible to get a hamburger and coke for twelve cents each. Everybody broke for lunch!

Except me! I slipped behind the door until everybody else was gone. The eye chart hung there before my eyes and I had thirty minutes to deal with it… which I did!

When we resumed after lunch, I read the first three lines of the chart for the Sergeant in record time, and he said, "O.K. get your clothes on and report to the Sergeant up front. He'll tell you when you will be leaving for boot camp.

I floated out of the recruiting office!

Then I looked down at the papers in my hand and it hit me—the not so pleasant task was ahead of me—breaking the news to my family and getting permission to do this!

My grandparents didn't exactly react with the joy I thought they would when I told them what I had done. "Does your Mother know about this?" were my grandmother's first words.

"No, but she will…soon as I get home."

I could hardly contain myself on the trip home. I walked up and down the ten train cars, constantly checking my enlistment papers, mentally practicing how I would present my case to my parents and get their signatures. The train had barely stopped when I hit the ground to walk the five miles to our farm.

There was no problem breaking the news to my Mother. My Grandmother had already called her on the phone, and she was ready with her response. "No! I won't sign those papers, Billy." She said. "We have one son already in the Pacific—in the Navy, and I won't sign for you to go…"

"Besides," she continued, "suppose I sign for you and you get killed." And she began to cry. This was the hardest part for me. She almost never cried.

I understood the possibility of what she feared, but I wasn't about to back down on my dream. I told her Dad would sign for me or—in typical teenage behavior—if I had to, I would get someone to sign their names for me.

My Dad signed the papers.

Three days later, I arrived by train at Parris Island, South Carolina for boot camp. I was on my way!

"When you pass through the waters, I will be with you...when you walk through the fire, you shall not be burned...For I am the Lord your God...and I am with you."

Isaiah 43: 2-4 niv

CHAPTER 6

BOOT CAMP

I ARRIVED AT Parris Island, South Carolina, a seventeen year old high school sophomore—right off the farm—never having traveled more than 200 miles away from my home. I was expectant, exhilarated, a little nervous, a little fearful…..

Fearful that the truth about my vision would be revealed, fearful—for I could not see well and had memorized the eye chart to pass the physical….

Fearful that my problem with reading would somehow surface. For example, if they gave me a test, I might not be able to pass it and they would issue me a train ticket and send me home.

These fears stayed with me, casting a dark shadow over my first few days.

Soon I was able to relax—somewhat. At least, I was at the Marine Corps Boot Camp. I was Marine recruit #561493 and it was time to see what I was made of.

Once boot camp training started, I found myself in a different world, a world I very much wanted to be a part of and was willing to work with all my strength and heart to be successful in it.

Reveille was sounded at five o'clock each morning. We had just a few minutes to be shaved, fully dressed and in formation. For about 12 hours a day the first five weeks, we were marching… marching… ma..r..c..h..i..n..g!! Among other things!

The heat factor in June and July in South Carolina was soaring around 100 degrees or better, with the humidity almost as high as the temperature. The uniform of every day was heavy dungarees and jackets. By mid-morning the dungarees and jackets were soaked with sweat. We'd spend the rest of the day marching in wet, sweat-soaked clothes, except for the rifle inspection time when we tore down our rifles for the drill instructor to inspect.

We'd begin to feel "out of it", but had to continue to march —sometimes not able to see the person in front of us. However, it was for sure that you'd hear the drill instructor—easily! He'd give a command, "to the rear, march", and you'd turn to go the other way, but you kept marching, you dare not stop— because if you fell out you'd be pulled over to the side of the parade ground to wait for a medic to get you to sick bay, and if you had to stay in sick bay overnight, the drill instructor would have you transferred to a new platoon. No one wanted to leave his platoon because the platoon soon became like family and every other guy a brother. So when you got so weak you thought you could go no further, you'd feed off the energy of the others around you. Their energy and determination and pride would enable you to get your second wind, or your third or fourth wind—whichever you happened to need.

The highlight of the day was Mail Call. That gave you a reason to keep going. Mail Call was every day after chow at lunch when we went back to the barracks. One day I received a package. When I opened it, I found chocolate chip cookies and a framed picture of my high school sweetheart, Dot.

Every package had to undergo the inspection of the drill instructor—who decided whether you could keep it or not. He referred to the cookies as "pogey bait" and I offered him one. He looked at the picture and he asked, "Does she have a sister?"

It was the first—and only—time the DI had ever indicated that I might be human—and that he was too! It gave me a good feeling about him. Up to then every word and action seemed to express the idea that he hated me—and the other guys. I was insecure, filled with fear around him. He kept telling me I was nothing and he was the only one who could make something out of me. When the platoon was at rest, he would go up and down the ranks as we looked straight ahead. One day his face appeared right before me—eyeball to eyeball! I had been careful to follow instructions. I had done nothing wrong—trying hard to do what I was supposed to. He said:

"So you're from Tennessee! I'm from Tennessee. You are a disgrace to the state. You are worthless. You'll never be a Marine."

DI's often carried sticks called "swagger sticks" twelve to 18 inches long. Sometimes as they yelled at you they'd punch you in the stomach with the stick, and they'd call you every name in the world they could think of—emphasizing how worthless you were.

Then they'd move on down the ranks to somebody else. He left me feeling completely "worthless". Everything he said was personal to me. In my mind I thought: "He's going to be watching me—everything I do—he's looking for a reason to kick me out, to make me fail boot camp." The fear I already had was increased immensely.

Especially when he made me sing the Yazamine song. Yazamine was a small place nearby without much merit as a town. He singled me out and had me sing—attempt to sing. The words went something like this:

I'm the stupidest Marine

From Yazamine

You've ever seen!!

It took a while for me to sort this all out. I had witnessed this routine as he did it to other guys. I now experienced it, I began to see it was a part of the process—impress on you whoever you were—or thought you were—before coming here, you aren't that person anymore. You're becoming a Marine. You're being molded into a Marine, part of a fighting machine designed to fight—and win!

THERE WERE ABOUT 75 to 100 in the platoon and yet we were all one. Further on in our training the DI (drill instructor) would tell us: "There is a reason for what you are experiencing here—what you learn here is what will keep you alive when you hit one of those islands in the Pacific". He was so right. There was a significant carryover from how you survived boot camp as to how you survived combat. I guess that was the reason there were so few Marines who dropped out in combat because the Platoon was molded together as one, like a family, and no one wanted to leave it.

Later on in combat I saw men who were hit and wounded and could have turned themselves in for a Purple Heart and a sure trip home refuse to do that, refuse to leave their post in the scene of battle. Their commitment to their country, to the job they considered so important, to the Corps, to their platoon—the guys they thought of as their brothers and comrades in arms—was so real that it raised a loyalty in them that was sure and binding.

I experienced that feeling after coming out of the trap at Chosin Reservoir when the temperature got to 40 or 50 degrees below zero. I could have turned myself into sick bay with frozen feet (frostbite). A few did. When that happened, you would be evacuated to Japan and sent back to the States, I knew I could do that because my feet were definitely frozen. But, quite honestly, the thought never took root in me because I knew I was there for a purpose and couldn't leave until that purpose was fulfilled.

After eleven week in Platoon 316 at Parris Island, Boot Camp was over. A special ceremony—graduation, I guess—was held in which we were issued our United States Marine Corps emblem to wear on the collar of our shirt and on our cap. The focus of my lifelong dream had become a reality. I was no longer a Private but a Private First Class. A Gung-Ho Private First Class, a bona fide United States Marine. Semper Fi was my battle cry! I had finally earned the right to proclaim it!

Pictures of Billy in and after Boot Camp

Out of the Trap ~ Billy DeVasher

"Commit your way unto the Lord, Trust also in Him, and He will bring it to pass."

Psalm 37: 5 niv

CHAPTER 7

WANDERINGS

NORMALLY WHEN BOOT camp was over, a Marine was sent from Parris Island to Camp Lejeune in North Carolina for advanced training before being shipped overseas. However, we were in a war and several platoons—#316 to which I belonged being one of them—boarded a train for a cross country trip to the Marine base in San Diego, California—Camp Pendleton.

The train had wooden, straight-back, bench-type seats, open windows for air conditioning, and no place to sleep but in the sitting position on the straight-back seat. The duration of the trip was five days, four nights. For each and every meal, we ate C-rations. C-rations were the food packaged and provided for those in combat. An average meal consisted of something like Spam, a small can of pork and beans, a cookie, and sometimes a small bar of chocolate. Since it was before the day of bottled water, we drank water from our canteens—warm water!

Once or twice a day the train would stop for us to get off, stretch, and do calisthenics. Then it was back on the train and full speed west. Our arrival at Camp Pendleton, was a very welcome event.

Our orders read that when we left boot camp, the destination was China where we would replace Marines who had been there for some time. Rumor had it that becoming a China Marine was a good thing, but after a few days these orders were changed. We would not be China Marines, a distinctive honor in the Marine Corps. We would instead get our traditional post-boot camp leave of 10 days.

That would have worked out well for me since my home was only a few hours from Parris Island, but the leave was great even though it meant traveling back across the United States for at least three days, spending three or four days at home, and making the three day trip back to California. In spite of the travel, it was great to be home for a while, and even greater to wear my uniform to school and around town. I would relish feeling like a Marine with a victory under his belt. Indeed, surviving boot camp made a guy feel like a victor!

I made it back a day before time to report in. Why not spend it in Los Angeles? At the Hollywood Canteen I'd heard so much about. This was a big indoor arena where the USO welcomed military personnel with refreshments, bands, music, dancing partners, and Hollywood stars who volunteered their time to come entertain the troops. I was lucky to be in the audience for two different radio shows (no television then) and to spend a day seeing some of the sights. For a 17 year old from the state of Tennessee, there was a lot to see and do.

After spending a night in the USO quarters in one of the bunk beds (free to military men) I hitchhiked back to Camp Pendleton and reported in with little time to spare.

SOON NEW ORDERS came. Our platoon was headed to the Marine Barracks in Honolulu, Hawaii. We boarded a ship for the voyage from California to the Islands which was not designed for 2000 mile trips over rough seas. It wasn't long into the 10/11 days that it took to get there until everyone on the ship was seasick—even the crew. It was the roughest boat ride you can imagine!

Added to the everyday sea sickness was the fact that there was nothing to do! There was one paperback book on board being passed around. I finally managed to get my turn at reading it. The book was FOREVER AMBER, a book everybody was talking about, a recent sensation in paperbacks. Reading about Amber was the only good thing about that trip!

I had been in Hawaii for a short time when I received a letter from my Mother telling me that my brother David, who was in the Navy, had come to the Naval station and would be in Honolulu several days. I took the letter and went to the company Commander to request permission to go to the Navy yard to see him. He gave me a pass, and I went—only to find that he had left for the States the day before.

IT WAS THEN that the best and worst of things happened. The best was that World War II was over and we had won! The worst: the war ended and I had not seen a minute of combat!

THE NEXT FEW months were a diorama of disappointment: training with no battle to fight, being assigned to a battalion with no destination, enjoying the fun and excitement of the Islands but knowing you weren't there for fun and that kind of excitement, being shipped back to the States—to Treasure Island—being processed, honorably discharged, and returned home. BACK HOME—BACK HOME TO WHAT?

There was a letdown to say the least! The letdown was unsettling! Where do I go now? What do I do?

I had completed my GED (Graduate Equivalency Diploma) while in the Marines and was officially a high school graduate. My high school coach urged me to come back, join the team and play football for a year, but that had no appeal to me. After all, what did I have in common with the high school guys now? It was more exciting to listen to my brother, Dave, who was going to the University of Tennessee at Martin to play college football. There was a spot for me on the team. They wanted me to come!

It did not register with me that I had only been to high school for two years and had done very little in the way of studying then—that I had actually never done much in the studying. The reality of college academics was just not for me! College was a place to learn, to read, to study. None of those were in my game plan. The main thing to me was that I was in great shape physically and could do well with the athletics. The fact that I was sorely disadvantaged in academics was a minor detail—of no significance to me!

MY FOOTBALL PROGRESS was sterling! My social life excelled! My studies not so much!

When the season ended, I was on the starting lineup of the football team—playing center on the offense and linebacker on defense, but my lack of background and interest in educational activities caught up with me. The social aspect of college was great, but I had no idea how to study and no interest in spending the time required to learn. I still thought I could fake it and bluff my teachers into thinking I was learning. Not so! I bombed out academically. I dropped out at the end of the semester!

BACK HOME AGAIN! I helped my Dad on the farm, I spent some time driving a truck delivering farm products, but I was restless and uninterested in farming. What to do now?

My Mother's sister, Aunt Lawton, lived in Lexington, Kentucky, home of the University of

Kentucky. Her neighbor was an assistant football coach there. Coach Ermal Allen—later with the Dallas Cowboys—suggested to her that I come by and try out for the team. Coach Bear Bryant was to become the head football coach there. I reasoned: "OK. Why not give it a try? This time," I said to myself, "It will be different. I will buckle down in the classroom and study."

My enrollment was not as a transfer, but as a high school graduate for the summer term of 1948. I was a freshman with a group of freshmen from all over the country. To be playing football for Coach Bryant was a big thrill. Early in the war, he had left coaching and gone into the Navy, where he served as a Navy Commander. That made him close enough to being a Marine for me.

Coach Bryant was brought to Kentucky to build a football team. They had been a basketball power house for a long time. Back then, regulations were that if a guy was good enough, he could come in the summer term and play on the team that fall. That was my hope. I did not have a scholarship and worked in the cafeteria to pay my way. They were generous enough to arrange my work hours around football practice schedule as well as classes.

I lasted one year at Kentucky and my grades caught up with me. For the second time, I gave up on football, and for the second time, I gave up on caring for much of anything!

BACK HOME AGAIN! Dave was still at UT Martin. All my friends were either off to college or working in a factory. I definitely was not interested in a career in a factory, so I went back to working with my Dad on the farm—for a while!

But there were no goals in my life. Restlessness took over—aimlessness. In my thoughts I searched desperately for what to do—and remembered two fellow Marines who talked glowingly of working in the wheat harvest in Oklahoma and Kansas. Why not hitchhike out there and try it out?

I threw a few things in a bag and hitchhiked to Oklahoma City, Oklahoma where my family had relatives that I had never met.

I arrived there late in the afternoon. Since I didn't know any of his name except the last one—since he was my Dad's brother—I figured there wouldn't be too many DeVasher's in the phone book—and I was right.

The one I reached was my cousin. I called him, introduced myself, and he invited me to spend the night with them. He and his wife and children picked me up, and we shared a good meal and fellowship together.

The next morning, I hitched a ride to Enid, Oklahoma, because my cousin told me there was a lot of wheat harvesting going on there. That afternoon I met a farmer in a restaurant who sent me to the grain elevator where farmers brought grain every day. There a man named John said, "I can use you. Come on."

He hired me on the spot, probably because I looked as if I could do heavy work, and took me home with him. His house was in the middle of what looked like miles and miles of wheat—in all directions all you could see was wheat waving in the wind.

His wife welcomed me along with another "hand" and sat us down to an evening meal of fried chicken with all the fixings.

John told me I would be paid when the harvest was completed. He said I would be paid in cash.

He knew nothing about me, but he took me to one of the bedrooms in his house. I knew nothing about them but I was really glad to climb into that bed and fall rapidly into a deep sleep.

Before daylight the next morning, we were called to breakfast. What a breakfast! Bigger than I'd ever eaten before! And we were off to the wheat field.

John drove the combine. We shoveled the wheat into a big truck—and I began to find out what real work was all about.

In the middle of the morning, His wife showed up carrying a big basket. It had plenty of water, more fried chicken biscuits, vegetables—another big meal—food that would stick to your bones, as they used to say.

At lunch, another big meal! At their house for this one. After that, a rest break—we stretched out under the trees in the yard. It was a pleasant respite and allowed us to regain some strength before we went back to the wheat fields. After a few days, I moved up to driving the tractor. One afternoon I missed my billfold. It had been in my back pocket and contained all of my assets—as little as they were. It must have fallen out of my back pocket as I worked. How in the world would I ever find it? I panicked! Parking the tractor, I started walking—back in the direction I had come—thinking I would never find it—not in a million years—not in this hundred acres of wheat!

I was wrong. In about five minutes of frantic walking and searching, there it was—lying in clear view, waiting for me to pick it up.

At that time, I wasn't thanking God for His watch care in my life. I wasn't even aware of it, but I should have been. Now I know that on this occasion—and many others—he actually worked miracles for this brash young man who had no idea of what he was doing or where he was going! He was so faithful to care for me when I was doing some pretty reckless things!

Losing things has plagued me often in my life. One time later in life when I was trading commodities in Chicago, I stopped at a pay telephone to make a call. The number was in my billfold. I was late, as usual. In a hurry! Down the road several miles, I missed the billfold, wheeled the car around and raced back, ran into the phone booth…and there it was! Lying exactly where I had left it.

I could tell you many, many other such incidents—but it would only bore you—and they would all have the same ending. Somehow, the unseen mercy and grace of a loving Heavenly Father was at work redeeming the time for me.

When we finished harvesting all the wheat, I left —leaving a family I came to respect deeply—a family who had provided me a great experience that summer and had rewarded me generously with money in my pocket worth the time I had spent there.

THE NEXT MORNING I was off to follow the wheat harvest through Kansas. I hitchhiked to Wichita, arrived late in the afternoon, walked around town, and settled down in a storefront hotel for the night.

About two o'clock in the morning I was awakened by a storm. Heavy winds were making a terrific noise. The next morning I walked down to find windows blown out, signs down, buildings blown down! After surveying the scene, I said to myself, "I don't believe I want any part of this. Maybe wheat harvesting is over for me."

And I started back to Tennessee!

Hitchhiking, of course.

AFTER CHRISTMAS IN the winter of 1948, restlessness overtook me again and I decided to hitchhike to California. I heard there was a lot going on there—jobs galore, plenty of adventure. Surely I, being 20 years old, could find my future and fortune there.

I took the southern route because it was winter, and I wore my college football jacket from the University of Tennessee at Martin—figuring it would be easier to catch a ride that way. People were open to picking up hitchhikers then—especially military men and college students.

Rides were good. The first day I made it all the way to Dallas, Texas, spent the night at the YMCA, I made the mistake of not sleeping in my UTM jacket—for it was gone. Somebody had stolen it during the night.

There I was—without a coat in the dead of winter—plus the jacket was helping me get rides. The big T on it led some to pick me up thinking it stood for the University of Texas.

The next stop was Kansas City where the YMCA was open like a barracks. It was Saturday night.

You're supposed to have fun on Saturday night, right? I found a very nice bar, a lounge, where the bartender told me of a dance a few blocks away, a good place to have a good time. I found it and stood around for a while. Everybody seemed to be having a good time. I thought: Why am I going to California? Two friends of mine, Billy Lane and Donald Reddick, had spent time in Peoria, Illinois, working at a Caterpillar Tractor plant. I could go there, get a job, and work for several months, save a little money, and see what happens next.

I changed courses! Found a city bus that took me to the edge of town, and headed to Peoria—hitchhiking, of course.

A snow storm was in progress. There I stood on the side of the highway in the middle of a snow storm—with no jacket—the roads frozen over—trying to catch a ride to a town I knew nothing about!

I was freezing!

I thought of going back to the YMCA and starting over when the weather got better. It seemed unlikely that anyone who would pick me up would be out in weather like this. The highway was a sheet of ice and snow.

And about that time, a car slowed down and stopped. The man inside was going to Chicago. Peoria was on his way. His car had a heater, a good radio, and he was a good conversationalist.

He dropped me off at midnight at the bus station in Peoria. Nothing to do but stretch out on a bench and sleep there until morning.

I was about to learn what the life of a factory worker was like: Find an upstairs room in a boarding house, have coffee and donuts at the corner store for breakfast, go to work at the second shift from 3:00 until 11:00 that night, and attend church on Sunday at the church across the street. It was o.k. I had a job, a place to sleep and eat, and go to church. Life was looking up! I even had a Saturday off when a friend invited me to go with him to Louisville to the Kentucky Derby. Not many months passed before the routine of this life became very boring to me, and I made my way back home in Tennessee

TWO FORMER MARINES had also returned to Portland: James Bryant and Jack Short. James had bought a small bulldozer, the kind used on Guadalcanal to clear air strips. It was a government surplus bulldozer that was avail for military veterans to buy.

He needed an operator for it and was happy to train me to run it. This was great for me, because he was one of my high school heroes. Not only that, but he had a beautiful new Chrysler convertible—white with red interior—sharp! He and his wife and another couple included me in their social life—me with my date for the evening, whoever that might be.

We all went night clubbing in Bowling Green, Kentucky, every Saturday night. This was about an hour's drive away. We partied and danced the night away. Just a fun time, I thought. I didn't have a car but he'd let me drive the convertible sometimes. I was occupied with the "life is a bowl of cherries" kind of life—running with James at night and driving the bulldozer in the daytime, plus going with them to Nashville for events, Vanderbilt football games and other interesting activities.

Another friend of mine, a former Marine, Jack Short, told me that James Elmer Payne was directing a Tennessee State Health Department X-Ray program on a mobile unit that moved from town to town taking chest X-rays of people. The purpose was to identify those who might have tuberculosis without realizing it. This disease, referred to as T B., was epidemic at that time and it was a killer. This sounded like a worthwhile job, something with some purpose to it—for even in the midst of my fun packed existence, I deep down knew there was more to life, and I definitely wanted more. I knew a person's life should have meaning and be spent in a way to help others—to make a difference for good as you live it. I somehow deep inside me knew that God was the Creator and Sustainer of life and that He had created us a purpose, a work to do and a relationship with Him to experience. Anyway, the traveling, staying in motels, eating good meals in good restaurants, meeting new people (especially girls) all the time also sounded very interesting and fun and that appealed to me very much.

I accepted the job—very happily!

Football practice at University of Tennessee at Martin

II.

FOX HILL

"Icon of the Korean War"

"No weapon formed against you shall prosper ...says the Lord."

Isaiah 54: 17

CHAPTER 8

FOX HILL

JUNE, 1950, ROLLED around with me caught in a web of wanderlust—just going where my whims—and the whims of others—pointed me. I was without purpose or meaning in my life—absolutely no direction in my life. Wherever the wind blew, that's where I found myself.

It was at that point that the North Korean People's Army attacked South Korea with surprising force. They succeeded in pushing deep into the country overtaking the capital city of Seoul and moving south in their attempt to take it over. The news went out immediately that the United States would be joining South Korea and the British Commonwealth—part of the United Nations—in sending military help to them.

I was elated! This was for me!

There was a Marine Reserve unit in Nashville with about 200 men in it. The call went out immediately that the United States Marine Corps was readying for immediate deployment to Korea. They needed men—especially men who had already gotten their feet wet in the Corps—those who had already been through boot camp and had experienced some of what going to war was all about! That was me!

The recruiting officer sent me directly to the C Company headquarters with instructions that I was ready for duty immediately.

The Marines were going to battle again, and I was a Marine. I would go with them! I who had absolutely no direction in my life would go with them.

When I went to re-enlist, I was welcomed with open arms. There was already a Marine reserve unit which had been training on weekends and going to summer camp. They'd earned the name of "weekend warriors", most of them having no idea they would actually be going to a real war. I joined them wanting to go to war, and quickly, became a part of this unit, C Company.

I was assigned as a machine gunner to a Weapons Company. Our squad leader was Sergeant John Henry. John and I became best of friends and even to this day, we still call to talk to each other. He received the Silver Star for his heroism on Fox Hill, but more than that, he saved my life on more than one occasion.

This Company C was the first unit to leave Nashville for the Korean War. On the day we left, we assembled at the Marine Reserve Headquarters, dressed in Marine Corps summer uniforms, boarded city buses to be escorted by motorized policemen to Memorial Square in downtown Nashville.

There we were honored with a send-off on the Tennessee capitol grounds in which the Mayor and other officials participated. Many family members were there to send us off. We were escorted again as we marched in formation from Memorial Square to Union Station where Dave and his wife, Ree, and my current girl friend, Patsy, and other members of the Marine's families waited to bid us good-bye. Families were experiencing a sad time because they knew where we were going and that we wouldn't be long getting there.

The train we boarded took us—once again for me—to Camp Pendleton, California.

We were assigned seats on the train—two guys facing two guys. We were in for a long hot ride from

Nashville to Oceanside, California, and Camp Pendleton.

A ride I don't remember many details about—it was boring and tiring and certainly not memorable in a good way! Even when you'd volunteered, you experienced a feeling of sadness for a while—you were leaving without a guarantee that you'd be back. But one memory stays with me. There were two guys—Marines—who had sneaked two gallons of moonshine whiskey on board. I had no idea how! They were drinking it in small paper cups—a little at a time—no sharing. They nipped on that from the time we left until it ran out. They seemed to feel no pain at all from the accommodations!

In California, reserve units were pouring in from all over the United States.. The Marine Corps at that time had the smallest number of men since World War II—approximately 450,000 men with only 75,000 on active duty.

In California, companies were being formed. The officers in charge were veteran leaders from World War II: Colonel Chester Pull (later a General), Colonel Homer Litzenbert, Colonel Ray Davis, Captain William Barber. These men had fought on Guadalcanal and others battles in that War and were decorated for their service there. Colonels Davis and Barber would receive the Congressional Medal of Honor for their part in helping free us out of the trap on Fox Hill. We felt good about their being our leaders because they were seasoned warriors.

The goal was to get us over there as quickly as possible.

The 7th Marine Regiment was formed and we shipped out of San Diego, California, headed to Korea aboard the USS Montrose. This ship was a troop carrier designed with bunks stacked six or seven high. Most of the time aboard the ship we were training because many of the guys had just graduated from high school and had been in Reserve units for a year, maybe two, but had had no real Marine Corps training. Consequently, some of them fired their weapons for the first time on a makeshift rifle range aboard ship.

We arrived in Kobe, Japan after the 15 day trip—a bit travel weary. Evidentially our leaders recognized that, for they granted us liberty—a leave from 3:00 in the afternoon to 10:00 that night. Dressed in uniform we were up and down the streets of Kobe—drinking Japanese sake (beer) served by Japanese waitresses. We went shopping too. I bought a Japanese kimono which I had shipped to Dot. I have no idea why I had it shipped to her since someone else had seen me off on this trip—but I did—and she still has it! Perhaps a foretaste of things to come.

After the short leave in Japan, we sped to the scene of battle and a rendezvous during high tide at Inchon Harbor where the real fighting began.

The INCHON LANDING was a big success. We joined other outfits there for General McArthur's famous Inchon Landing. History has recorded that action, which took place unexpectedly at high tide, as one of the greatest masterminded events in military history.

The liberation of Seoul, South Korea's capital city was next. This was a major battle requiring several hours of bombardment from many ships in the bay, lots of air power, and many Marines to do the ground work. My machine gun was set up on a hill overlooking Seoul. Navy Corsairs were flying so low over our heads that I thought they would surely take our helmets off. I did not know at that moment that my future brother-in-law, my wife's brother was the pilot in one of those planes. He helped free Seoul. He was hit—actually the bottom of his plane was destroyed so that he could look down and see the ground. He managed to pilot the plane into territory above the 38th parallel, crash land, survive, and become the first Navy pilot to be picked up out of enemy territory by helicopter in war time. He suffered a gunshot to his leg and a broken back—which he wasn't aware of until he was back on the ship.

After Seoul have been liberated and secured, the job was to push the North Koreans north, to drive them back beyond their borders. It took four months of intense fighting, four months of successful fighting. Now we were headed north to the Yalu River with the mission completed. South Korea would once again be free!

We had been told that once we reached the Yalu River, we would board ships and be on our way back to the States—home!

On our way north, we were ordered up a mountain to guard the Toktong Pass. It was there in the early morning hours—around two o'clock—that our Company was attacked by the Chinese Communists Army and cut off from the others.

From where I sat on that terrible November 27, 1950, it seemed to be anything but success. Except the success that some of us survived the onslaught of that first night's assault.

Morning came and with it the feeling that none of us may survive another night.

With the morning also came the daunting task of assessing the damage. How many wounded? How many suffering from frostbite? How many killed? And how many incapacitated by shock and fear? And of great importance, how much ammunition did we have left, for the enemy would surely come this night?

No one had any forewarning that we would be in 40 degree below zero temperature—even colder sometimes for the temperature would change as the wind came down the mountain in a funnel—making it as low as 60 degrees below zero. The big question was: how could we keep from freezing? We had been issued some cold weather gear, but nothing like enough for this weather. And some things we had were totally inadequate. For example, we had Q-shoepaks to put in our boots. The problem was that they worked for a few hours and then your feet would begin to sweat and the moisture would freeze. Now you had a frozen pack glued to your foot. You had to keep moving constantly to try to keep yourself, especially your feet, from freezing. In a foxhole that became difficult to impossible to do.

That first morning we started looking for sticks, branches, pine trees—anything with which we could build a fire. That didn't work. The order came as soon as the first fire was lit to put it out. It would give away our position.

No fires! Nothing to warm ourselves by.

We had to face reality! We were trapped! We were in sub-zero weather. Our ammunition was very low! We had almost exhausted the supply we had—firing many rounds. And our food was limited—we had very little in the way of C rations.! What would we do? How could we defend this Hill?

The first morning after the Chinese attacked, I made my way down the Hill from where my machine gun was set up to check on our supply of ammunition. A tent had been set-up for the dead and wounded Marines. After the third night, the bodies of the dead had to be stacked outside the tent because there was hardly enough room for the wounded. The stack of dead Marines began to grow as others were killed. You just brought them and added their bodies to the stack.

As I was down checking on the ammo, I noticed a circle of Marines sitting beside that tent. They were just sitting there—staring into space. Their weapons were with them. It was a scary, unusual sight to see. I had never seen anything like it. A term that was used back then was called the "bunkhead stares". That's what had happened to them. They were shell-shocked. They had lost it.

I thought, "Man, we need you guys here on Fox Hill to help fight off these Chinese". I didn't know what happened to that circle of men. I was too focused on trying to hold our position. Every day we had fewer guys to fight because during the night, some were killed, some were wounded, some were frozen. The numbers of able bodied fighters became fewer and fewer.

As I look back, I wonder how any of us survived. I don't know the answer to that. I was awarded the Silver Star for my action on Fox Hill. The citation said for bravery, but every man there during those five nights and six days was brave. When we landed at Inchon four months earlier, we didn't know what was ahead for us but I remember in those early days I knew I was where I was supposed to be and that if I got killed here and didn't make it home alive, then that would be o.k. because I didn't really have anything to go back to. If I died here, it would be for a good cause, a worthwhile thing to give my life for.

AS THE DAY wore on that first day, it was relatively quiet. The Chinese did their fighting in the middle of the night. We had to be ready for we knew they would be coming. We'd hear the bugles—small bugles they carried with them. They also had whistles. When you heard them sounding, you knew the assault was beginning.

Even though they usually fought at night, we could never relax, for during the day, there were constant snipers firing on us from every direction. We knew there were many, many of them there. And we knew that our number had been seriously decimated already. We did not know that there were 100,000 Chinese surrounding us and that another 100,000 were waiting in reserve to take their place. They were there firing on us night and day. We did know that they obviously did not know how few there were left of us. They could have wiped us out at any minute—but they didn't. We had excellent support—heavy artillery, bombardment. What a beautiful sound the first time I heard the compelling noise of the sound coming over my head, whistling through the air—a surprising but good sound. They had no air power at all. They just had men—

hundreds coming constantly in their cotton, quilted white uniforms (hard to see in the snow and ice) and cotton sneakers (hard to hear).

We could not allow ourselves to sleep—day or night. We were well aware of what could happen if you slept because of what we had seen on the way up Fox Hill. An advance team of eight Marines had been sent ahead to check out the lay of the land and prepare the way for the troops. As we moved up the Hill, we came across a spot when a couple of rows or sleeping bags were laid out on the ground. They seemed to be occupied. "What's going on here? This is strange."

We found out quickly. The eight Marines had laid out their sleeping bags, gotten in them, zipped them up to get some sleep and stay warm. The enemy had found them and bayoneted every one of them. They didn't have a chance!

Our Company Commander immediately sent out an order that no sleeping bags were to be zipped up.

The idea of a warm night's rest was gone. In its place was a feeling of helplessness at seeing what had happened to those guys. It also gave us more determination to get the Chinese who had done this to our fellow Marines. They never had a chance to fight. They had no knowledge that the enemy was that close; no warning or opportunity to get ready for action.

EARLY ON I began to pray my five minute prayer: "Lord, let me live for 5 more minutes". You learned early that these Chinese soldiers were there for one purpose—and one purpose only—to kill you! The Marine Corps never gave us any training on how to be a POW (prisoner of war). So you didn't have to wonder if you were going to be taken prisoner or not. You knew they were there to kill you! And you had to fight like Marines to the death to win this battle. Thinking like this was a result of the training of a Marine from boot camp on.

We began to worry more about our ammunition than about ourselves. We were rapidly using it up. What would we do when we ran out? We thought as long as we had ammunition we'd be able to defend our position—even against incredible odds. Without ammunition, we would be lost.

Then we were told to expect an air drop soon: food, ammo, warmer clothes, antifreeze for my water-cooled machine gun so it wouldn't freeze up in the 40 degree below zero temperature. We had to work with them constantly to keep them working.

That evening about dark (I'll never forget that day), we heard the planes coming. What a beautiful sound. They were flying so low and close to us that we could see the guys wave to us as they pushed the bundles out of the planes. For a moment I thought:

"Gosh, I wish I'd joined the Air Force. I'd be heading back to have a hot dinner and sleep in a warm bed—back where no one would be shooting at me."

We watched with glad anticipation as the supplies fell from the planes—and rolled into the ravine—right to the bottom of the Hill.

The Chinese had also seen the drop, and as we started after them, they were ready with their sniper fire.

We were able to retrieve about half the drop. The other half fell into enemy territory occupied by the Chinese. What a struggle to save what we could and get it back up the Hill—only to find that half of what we had retrieved was toilet paper! We had no need of toilet paper. It was too cold to go to the bathroom—there were no bathrooms; we couldn't even use the paper for fires.

That first day, we paid a lot of attention to our

foxholes. It was important to have one and that it be deep enough to provide some shelter. Sergeant John Henry, our platoon leader, and I were very fortunate to find an abandoned hole that had obviously been dug by the North Koreans at an earlier skirmish. It was big enough and deep enough for us not to get blown away with heavy artillery and bombardment.

There was no water on the Hill. Everything was frozen. Up in the morning of that first day as I looked over everything around me, I noticed a ravine at the bottom of the hill, a gully where that hill met the next one. I stood there and looked and said to myself, "It's possible there is a spring at the bottom of it and springs don't freeze."

I meandered around the side of the hill by myself, worked my way to the point where hill met hill and sure enough, there was running water. I couldn't get to the spring itself but a pool of water that had accumulated—not frozen over—fresh water! I lay down in order to get my face in the water, took off my gloves and braced myself to get far enough out to drink. A sniper from somewhere had seen me and keyed in on me. As I was lapping the water, I noticed the water move around me as if someone were throwing pebbles in the pool—ripples all around me—it was bullets—the sniper was firing at me and it was hitting the water—close to my head and hands and body.

My thought was: "You just keep shooting, pal! I'm going to drink all the water I want."

I didn't try to get up—run—hollow or scream. I just said, "Keep shooting. I'm going to get a drink of this water." At the time, I wasn't worried about getting shot. I seemed to be insulated in a cocoon of resignation and determination. I just wasn't worried about getting hit or killed. There was a job to do and I was there to do it. Making my way back to my machine gun, my thought was that whatever is to be is to be. Sergeant Robershaw, a professional Marine who had seen service for seven or eight years, joined Sergeant Henry and me in our foxhole. Sergeant Robershaw was famous for saying things like, "All the rest a Marine needs is just sixteen seconds, and he's ready to go again." He was also an expert marksman who had taken a bolt action rifle from the body of a Chinese soldier. It had a scope on it. As we sat on the side of the embankment where my machine gun was, looking out over the snow covered mountains, he handed me his field glasses and said: "DeVasher, see those Chinese on that hill over there; spot them for me! I want to see if this rifle is as good as it's supposed to be." He fired and one fell . . . then another . . . and another. He was so pleased with himself. I handed the field glasses back to him and moved away. I thought that those men weren't bothering us at the time—and I'm not going after them unless they start blowing their bugles, and coming up the ravine with their weapons firing—trying to get me!

Time in combat hardens some men to the point where they like to kill. Others of us carry out orders, do what you have to do, just try to stop the enemy and protect the innocent.

THE TRUTH WAS that had Fox Hill not been defended the Chinese Communists could have been successful in their march south and taken the country. They just didn't know how few guys we really had up there, how outnumbered we were.

After that first drop, it was worked out and supplies that we needed were dropped for us. The Navy Corsair pilots flew so low that you felt you could almost reach up and touch the wings of the planes.

In the July 3-16, 2000, edition of the Stars and Stripes magazine, Shelley Davis wrote an article about this event in Marine Corps history. The article says:

"Resupplied and reinvigorated, the men of Fox Company maintained their position night after night in minus 40/50 degree temperatures. "Marines had never fought in that kind of weather," DeVasher said, recalling one man who sported a prized handlebar mustache. "It was so frozen, it would have broken off if anybody touched it.

On the second night, the Chinese began urging the "brave Americans" to surrender. One of the Chinese spoke in masterful English through some kind of pipe from the next hill over. (His voice rang out loud and clear across the cold night air. He told us they had us out-numbered and that we should surrender; that they would give us warm clothes and hot food, and a warm place to sleep . . . "We have you surrounded . . .You are about to be annihilated" . . . and on and on he went!

You can imagine the Marine response to that! It wasn't in a language that is acceptable to the ears of most of the readers of this account! Surrender is not a word in the vocabulary of Marines! And the mention of it has exactly the opposite effect! It really fired up the guys to make a stand and fight their way out of this mess! Every night the Chinese repeated their offer. It just "stiffened the Marines' resolve to stick it out" with a view to escaping from the trap the Chinese thought they had created.

The Chinese soldiers wore white insulated uniforms and white caps. They were hard to see and to hear in their cotton sneakers. They knew how to move like mice coming up the ravine, up the slope like animals sneaking up on their prey. We were trying to win the war with air power and mortars. They were trying to win with just men, hundreds, thousands of them coming four abreast. They came and kept coming.

If any were to survive, to escape, Fox Company's rapidly diminishing number needed help. "By December 1, General Edward Almond, the X Corps commander, realized that Fox Company had to be evacuated if any of them were to survive. An attempt to reach the unit on November 29 already had failed after encountering strong enemy defenses. The next day, Major General Oliver Smith, commander of the First Marine Division, ordered the Fifth and Seventh Marines to move out toward Fox Company on Toktong Pass.

"The Fifth Marines thus marched into one of the unsung sagas of the Korean War, trudging through the night across frozen hills led by Lt. Col. Raymond G. Davis. As temperatures fell to 20 to 30 degrees below zero, the trail became packed with ice. They fought off exhaustion.

At 11:30 p.m. December 2, they reached Fox Company, halting only long enough to pack up the dead and wounded and destroy equipment that had to be left behind. Fewer than 30 of the 240 men who had marched up Toktong Pass were able to walk down.

"After six nights on top of the hill, Fox Company's ordeal was only half over, but they had survived the worst.

The trek to the ships waiting to evacuate them south was more than 70 miles distant along twisting, narrow dirt roads. As they moved out, refugees streamed behind, trying to cross bridges before the Marines blew them up.

"It took until December 11 for the last elements of the First Marine Division to reach the safety of Hungnam Harbor.

We had to fight our way out of the trap. The first eleven miles were especially treacherous for we came over the ridge and hills—not by way of a road. The road had to be kept clear. We climbed up and down one mountain after another, never knowing where the enemy was hiding and when they would strike. We lost some men and others were wounded even as we moved out—the question always in our minds of who might be the next. Our equipment had to be left behind. There were just men with their machine guns and mortars. We knew that an Army Unit had been decimated at the eleven mile mark. We didn't want a repeat of that event. It was with determination, hope, and the built-in belief that Marines don't give up—that some of us finished the 70 mile trip to the boat that would take up south out of the trap!

1. THE KOREAN PENINSULA BEFORE HOSTILITIES, MAY 1950

Out of the Trap ~ Billy DeVasher

Korean War—Fox Hill

Out of the Trap ~ Billy DeVasher

"The faithful love of the Lord never ends! His mercies never cease. Great is His faithfullness; his mercies begin afresh each morning"

                    Lamentations 3: 22-23 nlt

CHAPTER 9

HOME AGAIN

FOX HILL WAS behind us—but not Korea. We finally made our way south from Fox Hill—still fighting the Chinese who seemed to be everywhere—and unfortunately losing more men. Those of us who were left finally boarded a ship at the Wonsan Harbor which took us to South Korea. We regrouped and waited for replacements for the men lost—new men from the States. The company needed to be rebuilt to its former strength. There was still front line combat for the next several months, but in

August, my time there was up. I was on my way home!

We left Korea in August, 1951 and landed in Hawaii to take on fuel. After lunch, they gave us leave with instructions to be back by 8:00 p.m. The ship would be leaving promptly at eight o'clock. Most of the Marines showed up somewhat sober. We had all been celebrating. It was a time to celebrate—being alive and in that beautiful place and on our way back to the United States, the finest country in the world. The feeling was exhilarating. It was my first real assurance that the war was over. At least for me, it was! I had survived—against incredible odds—a year I would never forget!

For many years afterward, I could remember every day of my entire experience during that year—almost every minute. I didn't need a calendar or a clock. It was that vivid in my mind.

For now, it was so good to be walking down the

street in Honolulu, feeling so free. No one shooting at you—no mortars dropping—your hands and feet not freezing—none of those concerns. I was safe! And free! I recalled the phrase that Jesus had said and understood its meaning in a new way: "...you shall be free—free indeed!" That was why we'd been here—to set the people of a captured country free! What a good thing it was to know—Mission accomplished!

The ship pulled anchor at exactly 8:00 and we left Pearl Harbor. Destination: California—the good ole USA! Home!

With almost everybody aboard! There were two guys—Marines—who didn't make it back to the ship in time. We all wondered about them. We were so eager to get home—we wouldn't take a chance on missing the boat. I never knew what happened to them. They could have been court martialed—maybe not—maybe they just caught the next ship to California! I hope so!

When we docked at San Diego, we were given a thorough physical at the distribution center. That was a delay none of us wanted. Especially me! For I did not pass the physical, which was not surprising considering my living conditions for the past few months!

I was sent to a holding center to be treated and tested every day until I was clear. It took several days but the medicine finally worked and I was honorably discharged!

The bulletin board had a notice from a civilian who was driving east as far as Kentucky and had room for three Marines. Just what I needed. He picked us up at the Marine Barracks and it was non-stop all the way—day and night. He let me out in Russellville, Kentucky, where my younger brother, Joe, was waiting to meet me. In less than an hour, I was home.

I was alive, well, out of that trap and more than ready to put it all behind me and get on with my life.

How happy I was to be back home in Tennessee! Home!

III.

FOR EVERYTHING THERE IS A SEASON…"

Ecclesiastes 3: 1

"I am confident of this: I will see the goodness of the Lord in the land of the living. Wait for the Lord; be strong and take heart and wait for the Lord.

Niv

CHAPTER 10

ENDINGS AND BEGINNINGS

HOME! TO AN era of endings and new beginnings.

It was the ending of life as I had always known it with Dad and Mom in the place that was home to me, for my Dad was very sick. His battle with the effects of his war injuries was coming to an end and he died a short time after I came home from Korea. He had suffered constantly for thirty-five years as a result of the damage done to his lungs and kidneys from being gassed in World War I at the Battle of Argonne Forest. He had lived through the depression years, taking care of his family, working for the railroad, doing duty as a law-enforcement officer, and running the farm on which we lived. As painful as it was to give him up, it was so good that I could be there with my Mother during those days.

It was the beginning of: How do I make a living now? What should I do?

When I knew I was going to make it out of Korea alive, I began to think I could farm for a living. I wanted to settle down. Dave said he would help me. I found a farm to lease. I had a little money saved with which I bought a Farmall tractor to get started. I bought several angus cows with the intention of developing a herd of cattle. For several months, it seemed it might work out. Until one day I called my Sergeant Major John Henry, who lived in Nashville. Just to touch base—see what he was doing and how he was making it.

John was traveling, selling automobile products. He said. "Come see me. There's something I want to talk to you about. Can you come tomorrow? Meet me at the Hillsboro Diner."

There is a bond of togetherness that develops between men who have spent time in combat together. I realized how much I had missed John Henry. We were friends of the kind that Jesus spoke of when He said, "Greater love has no one than this, than to lay down one's life for his friend." We had both experienced that.

He told me about his job and what great money he was making. I expected the next thing John was going to say was, "Bill, you can do this too. The company will hire you."

But he didn't. He said, "Bill, do you remember Lt. Zorn, our platoon leader in South Korea? He's now Captain Zorn, the company commander of our old C Company in Nashville. He's been assigned to get the company back to full strength. Most of the guys who survived Korea got out of the Corps when we got back. He has to recruit new men. He needs help and wants me to come on his staff as a Recruiting Sergeant. Listen—I think I'm going back in the Corps. Would you like to come with me? There's need for another Recruiting Sergeant. It will be great duty!"

Suddenly farming seemed slow and laborious and boring and the door was open for me to join John Henry recruiting guys for the Marine Corps. I didn't hesitate. My reply: "It sounds great to me. I'm ready." I was back on active duty with the Marines again.

I sold my entire farming operation to Dave, my brother who loved everything about farming, with a "Pay me when you can" agreement. I walked away from farming. It wasn't for me! I was a Marine recruiter and having a great time doing it!

THERE WAS ALSO another new beginning, a renewed relationship with Dot. We rekindled the coals that were left from our dating days back in high school. During that eight year span, we had gone our separate ways. We managed to see each other when she and I were both in town. I would call her and we would catch up on a "what are you doing now?" type of date.

Both of us had dated others during that time, and both were in a "maybe we'll get married" relationship with someone else when I left for Korea—but the circumstances of the past few months had changed us both. I had to face my own mortality on Fox Hill. She had a serious car accident which left her immobilized for several months. We both had time to think about our lives and what we would do with them. Her note to me in Korea told me how glad she was that I had survived Fox Hill. It was a friend-to-friend correspondence. I wrote her back and soon it was anything but a friend-to-friend relationship. When I arrived home from Korea, I hugged my Mother and Dad, set my seabags down, and headed to south Mississippi where Dot was working.

There is no doubt in either of our minds that the vows we made to each other at the altar on December 20, 1952, were meant to be. We realized deep down inside that God had a direct hand in bringing us back together, and that His guidance, his input into our marriage has resulted in the 60 years of marriage we have shared with each other, and with the family we treasure: 3 children, 3 children-in-law whom our children married, 6 grandchildren, two grandchildren-in-law who have married two of our grandchildren—and now two great grand-children. The extensions on the dining table are long and longer each year and the Christmas Eve all night party—with everyone sleeping over in anticipation of Christmas morning—gets bigger and bigger and more meaningful as time goes by.

There is no doubt about it. God knows what he is doing when he brings change into our lives.

December 20, 1952

Billy and Dot exiting church after wedding in 1952

"Do not be afraid, nor be dismayed; be strong and of good courage—for the Lord thy God is with you wherever you go."

Joshua 10: 25 nkjv

CHAPTER 11

A SEASON OF BLESSINGS

AFTER DAD DIED, my Mother moved in with her aging parents to care for them. They lived a short distance from her house. She suggested that Dot and I could move into her house after we were married—since it was empty. We renovated it: new paint, new wallpaper, refinished floors—making it our new home and we began our new life together, a wonderful time as well as one of adjusting to marriage—to living with each other.

This adjustment was more easily said than it was done. As God sometimes does, He had brought two people together—very, very much in love with each other—but very, very different in many of our ways. It was a new adventure for sure! An adventure which has continued every day for the last 60 years and continues to this day.

We began to find out that God has a sense of humor and a plan for each of our lives, just as He said in Jeremiah 29: 11, "a plan to give us a hope and a future that is good"…and sometimes surprising!

That plan didn't include our living in Portland, as much as we loved this place where we had grown up, where we had friends and relatives galore. I was still assigned to recruiting duty for the Marines and still stationed in Nashville. Dot's teaching job in a nearby community called Westmoreland had come to a halt with the end of the school year, and in our sharing and growing closer together, we found our goals, dreams and aspirations for the future were the same —to make our lives count for something positive.

Although, up to this point, my life had had little or no direction, I now found it filled with purpose and a desire to live it in a worthwhile way.

Dot and I had known each other for a long time. It had been eight years since our first date in high school. She knew of my love for the Marines and of my frustration with the classroom. She knew I had wandered through three different schools without success. She did not know that I was deeply disappointed with myself because I had given up and felt like a failure because of it. She did not realize that I wanted a college degree intensely. That desire surfaced as we talked on our way home from our honeymoon. She simply replied that it wasn't too late to remedy that situation if I really wanted to pay the price it would take to correct it. That was all that was said about that. However, a seed of possibility, of hope was planted in my mind.

But how could that happen? There were so many things we had to do now—wanted to do now. The fact was that I was greatly limited in academic ability from neglect and misuse. The odds of my having success were against me. I recalled the trap at the Chosin Reservoir in Korea. The feeling of my being surrounded and cut off, trapped in a situation of my own doing overwhelmed me. Whatever the reason, the idea of doing something about it, of escaping the lack of education trap, went on the back burner for the time being. a dimly burning light, glimmering only slightly and threatened by extinguishment. When a person is seemingly hopelessly trapped, it is difficult to find the courage to reach for freedom, even less to fight for it. Difficult but not impossible!

At this point in my life, I was just beginning to learn through experience that "with God, all things are possible." I was to find out about his grace and mercy in amazing ways as time went on.

Several months later, we moved to Nashville. Our first child was on the way and we had to make a life for her as well as for ourselves. So we bought a little two bedroom house on Wildview Drive in Nashville. I had been driving there every day since Marine headquarters were there and I was still on active duty. Actually this house seemed to just fall in our laps. It was a new house that the supply Sergeant at the Marine Reserve Headquarters had bought less than a year before—not knowing that he was going to be transferred so soon. One day he told me about it and said: "Billy I want someone to take over the loan and begin with the next payment." A house available to us in a perfect location, close to the recruiting center—an ideal place—and the monthly payments were $58.00 a month—a cozy, comfortable, convenient, attractive home for $58.00 a month!

Our first child, a daughter, Terry, arrived in September, 1952, and we became a family. Nothing motivates a man more than the responsibility of this new little person who was completely dependent on you. It was definitely time for me to get serious about the path our lives would take. A new direction was needed that would require several changes on my part. I was ready to face those changes—wanted to face them.

THE FIRST CHANGE would have to be in my educational status, the idea simmering on the back burner of my mind would have to be brought to the front—to a full boil. I had long realized that I was caught in a trap that was limiting me greatly because of the educational deficiency I had. It seemed wise—

even expedient—to do something about that. I would begin in a small way with night classes.

Since I loved to talk and was pretty good at it, I decided to start off with a speech class at the University of Tennessee extension center in Nashville, a night class.

The class went well and I found that being on my feet in front of people—talking—was pleasing to me and something that I was good at. That would later be a strong asset in my favor.

ALONG ABOUT THIS time I discovered that I had another challenge. Another area of my life in which I was seemingly trapped emerged. It had not been a major problem until I became a Marine and the habit intensified then and—as nicotine does—gained its hold on me until I was smoking something like three packs a day. I had fallen into the nicotine trap and it had a strong, firm grip on me. It had to go, I bit the bullet and on New Year's Eve of 1954, I smoked my last cigarette. I had tried to "smoke my last cigarette" numerous times before that day but without success. I was beginning to see what Jesus had meant when He said, "You will know the Truth and the Truth will set you free." Even though my relationship with the Lord was not very strong at that time, I still believed that there was a power available through Him that could break chains that enslaved people. Taking that road to freedom with Jesus and his power set me free—that and chewing a whole lot of gum and toothpicks!

He said, "I am the ...Truth" and "you will be free indeed". It is the truth that I have never touched another cigarette to this day!

I was so glad and so relieved to be free of that habit, that addiction—glad to be out of that trap. I have a very close friend who today smokes three to four packs of cigarettes a day—as I did then. If I were still smoking today, as he is, I would not have the energy to work out at the gym a few times a week as I do now at 85 years of age. I would not want to live with the fact that smoking is no longer acceptable as it was. Everybody who was anybody in those days smoked. I don't want to get on a soap box. I believe everybody has a right to live as they wish, to smoke if they wish even though it is very destructive to them. My friend has emphysema and has been told by his doctor that he needs to quit or else he will one day smother to death. Life is much too precious and too challenging to watch it go up in smoke!

"You have been called to one glorious hope for the future. There is one Lord...and one God and Father, who is over all and in all and living through all."

Ephesians 4: 4-6 niv

CHAPTER 12

OUT OF THE TRAP OF "NO EDUCATION"

IN THE SPRING of that year, 1954, I enrolled in Belmont College, paid my tuition, but ended up not attending once again, there was that loathing of knuckling down to study.

Actually, I just didn't know how to do it!! I had avoided it like the plague for much of my life. Now I stood face to face—a formidable enemy separating me from something I wanted with all my heart!

I had gotten out of the Marine Corps by now and we had moved to Murfreesboro, Tennessee, to open up an office to sell Amana Food plans. The idea was if people bought an Amana Freezer, the company would fill it up with food at wholesale prices as a bonus and an incentive to buy. Then the company wanted an office opened in the Waverly, Tennessee, area and so we lived there part of the time.

A YOUNG EVANGELIST named Billy Graham had burst onto the national scene in 1949 when he conducted a revival meeting in a tent out in Los Angeles, California. That tent came to be referred to as "The Canvas Cathedral". The meeting continued for weeks, and numerous Hollywood personalities began making decisions for Christ, including Stuart Hamblen, famous then for his LA radio shows and his race horses. After his decision, he sold his race horses, quit gambling, and wrote famous song hits including "It Is No Secret What God Can Do" and "This Old House."

Jim Vaus, an electronics expert and wire tapper for the notorious gangster, Mickey Cohen, was among the converts. Jim spent the remainder of his days preaching the Gospel through amazing displays of electronic energy and finally became president of Houghton, a Christian college up east.

Dr. Graham's spectacular success was spurred on by the media. William Randolph Hearst, the publishing mogul who owned scores of prominent newspapers across the nation, sent all of his editors a command: "Puff Graham", meaning to publicize him thoroughly. Little did Hearst, not known for being religious at all, realize how God had employed him to help establish possibly the greatest evangelist since the Apostle Paul.

I am one of the millions throughout the earth who was strongly influenced by Billy and his team. By 1954 he had preached a number of what he called "Crusades "across America. In the summer of '54, he was invited to Nashville where he conducted a crusade in Vanderbilt University football stadium.

Although I had joined the Methodist Church when I was thirteen years old, I genuinely met Christ for the first time during the Nashville Crusade. I was supposedly making calls to sell Amana Food Plans, but one night was slow and I was drawn to the stadium just to see what was going on.

Strangely moved, I went the next night—and the next, taking my wife with me this time. Decades later, I still remember one of his favorite phrases: "God can put a smile on your face, a spring in your step, and joy in your heart It doesn't matter where you've been or what you've done, Christ's presence in your life can make all the difference." Not only did I accept Christ's redeeming grace that night, but the Lord made a special claim on my life—to follow Him and to preach to others about Him.

Pastors counseled me that night and said, "Billy, if God has called you to preach, then it's necessary for you to prepare for it. Even though Paul was a learned rabbi, after God called him, he spent three years being taught by the Lord in the Arabian desert." Needless for me to note, God had not summoned me to the Arabian desert, even though I would have happily gone, but I recoiled from the thought of studying to prepare myself. After all, I had made the rounds—UTM, UK, Western Ky, only to strike out every time What were the odds that I would succeed this time?

But—off I went to talk with the dean at Belmont (then Belmont College, now University). He was brutally candid with me. He exclaimed, "Billy this is the worst transcript I've ever seen!"

With much reservation, Belmont accepted me on "on probation" They desperately needed students. My future depended on what I did that first semester.

Dr. Dewey Roach was on the faculty and became a source of incredible help and support. Dot and I had previous ties with him because he had been her pastor and I, being an independent sort of guy, was about to learn one of life's important lessons. We can't make it by ourselves. Our only resort was to swallow our pride and call on God which, believe me, I learned to do—often and loudly. It was also very helpful to have a few friends like Dr. Roach in your corner. With everybody on deck—including the Almighty—I made it through that first semester.... and the second. and the third and before my educational experience came to an end, I had earned a Bachelor of Science degree, a Master's Degree, a Specialist in Education, degree from Vanderbilt-Peabody University and a Doctorate in Theology from Luther Rice Seminary..

Against all odds, the Heavenly Father had motivated and equipped me to accomplish more than I had ever dreamed of.

But not without the help of a whole lot of people along the way, such as the speech teacher whose class I enrolled in my first semester at Belmont College. She play a significant role in my journey out of the "trap of no education". She was Professor Marjorie Bunyan who was teaching while her husband earned a Ph.D. degree at Vanderbilt University.

She was very intelligent as well as a person with a lot of compassion and interest in her students. She taught Theater, Drama and Basic Public Speaking, a prerequisite to the Argumentation and Debate class which I really wanted. I knew I really needed this class because of preparing for the ministry—to which I had committed my life. I wanted to be the best preacher that I could be.

Belmont, at the time, was a small, conservative denominational College. I didn't think my background—coming out of the Marine Corps and serving in two wars over a period of some 8 years would be a good resume for a Christian college. I had a lot of apprehension about that, as well as the fact that I was 10 years older than most of the other students there—plus many of their backgrounds were from church related occupations: youth ministries, summer camp programs, local church occupations and activities. They were pretty well prepared for what they were coming into.

I felt really out of place. Mrs. Bunyan helped me bridge the gap. I remember her saying to me more than once, "Mr. DeVasher, you just need to learn this. I know you can. I will help you." And she did.

My greatest source of help came from my wife, Dot, who often worked into the night to help me get my assignment ready for the next day. Often, when I wanted to throw my hands up and quit, she would say, "No, we'll work this out." And we did!

Dot believed in me more than I believed in myself. She had a ten year head start on me since she became a real believer in Christ early in life, and I was just beginning to find out the truth about Him and what He wanted for me. I found I needed to believe in Him and also in myself, but I also believed in Dot—who really believed that a person "could do all things through Christ Jesus who gives the strength." (Philippians 4: 13) I also believed in her—that with His help and guidance we could—and would—work it out and do whatever needed to be done. That belief in the Lord has worked for us for many years. It started back then when we needed it most. It continues in full force today. He has been our "refuge and strength" in every situation we've faced.

IT WASN'T LONG before I got an invitation from a church to become their pastor and she got a job teaching in the public school in Nashville. I was also selling door to door. We were able to make it financially.

"Seek first the Kingdom of Heaven and all these blessings shall be added unto them."

Matthew 6: 33 niv

CHAPTER 13

MORE SHOWERS OF BLESSINGS

SUDDENLY MY SCHEDULE was packed and overflowing. There were classes in the mornings. Afternoons and evenings were spent working to make a living, studying whenever and wherever it could be worked in and through it all, God was present and exceptionally good to me and my family.

To this day the Nashville area is packed with preachers wanting a church. I was one of them. Almost right away, I began receiving invitations to preach on the weekends. My focus was not on money. That was no concern for a guy who desperately wanted to preach. At times, the churches where I preached were financially generous. At other times, I received nothing, not even gas money, but it didn't matter. The opportunity to speak to others about my growing relationship with the Lord Jesus Christ was compensation enough.

Soon the door was opened for me to become the pastor of the First Baptist Church in Westmoreland, Tennessee. We soon moved to this small community, about an hour from Nashville, to pastor this small congregation. It was o.k. for it to be small because I was now part of a church and I was motivated to believe that it wouldn't be small long. There was a lot to be done: visiting, talking to people about their lives and what the church could do for them, getting to know everybody in town.

My wife had been a teacher in that community before we married and she already knew a lot of people there. We moved to an older farm house in serious need of repairs and modernization, but that was all right too.

Since I was still in school at Belmont, that meant catching a Trailway bus every morning before daylight, getting to Nashville a little more than an hour later, taking the trolley to Belmont and rushing to be in class by eight o'clock. Every evening I returned home by bus after dark. Dot met me at the bus.

As I mentioned, the membership of the church was small—my salary was even smaller—but it was all sufficient—and somehow we made it never worrying about what we had—and certainly what we didn't have. I was happy to approach pastoring it as if it were the biggest church in all Christiandom. It was enough to be involved in the greatest and most meaningful work we could imagine. Our days were happy and fulfilled and the church grew in both numbers and spiritual strength.

AFTER MY EARLY hatred of studying subsided (I actually learned to read and to enjoy it), I graduated from Belmont with a B.S degree (Bachelor of Science) in June of 1957—my first degree.

Several miracles had taken place to bring me to that place and I was well aware of it. Our hearts were full of thanksgiving and excitement. We had to celebrate—to reward ourselves for a job well done. The reward: a "luxurious" trip to Florida—a four day, three night vacation in the sun and sands of Panama Beach. We still remember the pleasure of that time and the total cost—a whopping one hundred ($100.00) dollars—and a pretty good sunburn!

In the fall of 1957, I enrolled in the Southern Baptist Theological Seminary in Louisville, Kentucky. We bought a two bedroom mobile home (which most people called a trailer) and moved it into a "trailer park" in Louisville, Kentucky. There were other seminary students with families living there. We were expecting our second child; a boy named Al. Space was becoming a big factor in our lives.

Fortunately my brother, Joe, was changing jobs and had to move. He needed a mobile home where he was going. We needed more room. We traded. He moved the mobile home to Indiana and we lived in his house until he sold it. When he did, we settled into an apartment in Seminary Village, an apartment community for ministers and their families who were in the same situation as we were.

Every weekend, we drove to the Baptist Church in Hickman, Tennessee. It was a 400 mile round trip. I would preach for the morning and the evening services, and spend the afternoon in the home of one of the members. The drive back after the evening service meant getting home in the wee hours of the morning. I had to be in class at 8:00 on Monday, prepared and ready to go in a discussion of the theology of men like Barth, Brunner, Tillich, Kierkegaard, and others who were leaders in the world of theological thinking. Imagine how sharp my mind was at that point.

After classes each day—including subjects like Greek and Hebrew languages, (even though I had trouble with English) I would go to my teaching/coaching job at Ornsby Village, a residence home and school for troubled children and teenagers.

On Sunday, February 2, 1958, we woke to a beautiful blanket of snow—8 inches to be exact. No traveling for that day. Nobody was going to travel that day. I would definitely not be going to preach in Tennessee. What a blessing that turned out to be. It was actually another miracle in our lives. It was assurance to us that the Lord had His hand on our lives for that day our son, Matthew Alexander, Al to us, entered our world. Had it not been for the paralyzing snow storm, I would have been 200 miles away in Hickman, Tennessee, with no hope of being there for his birth. We learned along the way that God does have a plan and is able to work that plan to our good when we turn things over to Him and just trust Him.

ORNSBY VILLAGE, where I was teaching and coaching, was a residential institution for youngsters who were sent there by the court. Many of them had been in trouble with the law. Most were from dysfunctional families whose parents were in prison or whose mothers were prostitutes. Some had been members of gangs and who attempted to create their own gang when they came to Ornsby Village. It was my job to teach them and it was good to get to coach them in basketball, especially when the team got to play in a tournament at Freedom Hall in Louisville.

I had trouble, however, with the lackadaisical concept of discipline there. By November, 1958, I had had enough and decided we would leave Louisville and the Seminary to pursue a different approach to the educational pathway that I needed to be traveling.

We found a small apartment in Green Hills in Nashville close to the Vanderbilt-Peabody academic opportunities.

The challenges we were facing were huge: Get admitted to Vanderbilt-Peabody for graduate school, find a job that would put food on the table for a family of four, and hope and pray that there was a church in the area that needed a pastor and would want me to be that pastor!

Miracles! I was accepted to the graduate school program and got a door-to-door specialty sales job, and on a warm spring day, a pulpit committee showed up at our front door—unexpectedly. This pulpit committee (they call them pastor-search committees now) was from the Barton's Creek Baptist Church in Lebanon, Tennessee. I think committees used to show up unannounced to see prospects in everyday situations to know what they were really like. Perhaps hoping to catch the preacher, his wife and kids in an unpreacherly predicament, maybe in the middle of an argument or with the preacher's house in disarray.

You guessed it! Our apartment was so small that the only place my wife could set up an ironing board was in the living room near the front door. It was a pleasant spring day and she had the door open to enjoy the beautiful weather as she ironed—in her shorts, of course! She had no choice but to greet them—in her shorts!!

She was mortified and thought she had blown any hopes of their being interested in her husband as a pastor. (You'd have to understand Baptist culture in that day to understand her concern.) But, not to worry. I preached a so-called "trial sermon" for Barton's Creek the next Sunday and they called me as their pastor.

The church provided a house, the pastorium, next to the church for the pastor and his family to live in. About a week before we were to move in, we drove over to see the house. It was in a beautiful setting surrounded by cedar trees. We walked in the house. There were hardwood floors, a big kitchen—you could have put our whole apartment in the living room space. They had just finished painting. We knew because the buckets and brushes were still there. We sat down on the buckets and thought another miracle had happened. We looked forward to living and serving in that community.

We moved into the pastorium next door to the church building in record time. Most of the congregation had grown up in that community but worked in town. They still came back to go to church at Barton's Creek. Soon the attendance filled the building.

In addition to a house, the church provided a small salary. The church was very conservative and so was the salary. It would have been fine except I was in graduate school. Not only did I have to pay tuition, but I had to buy gas and keep my old car running. I drove to school 3 times a week, and did the traveling necessary to pastor the church. I asked my wife how we made it. She said she had no idea, but she did know money was really tight. One Christmas, I was asked to speak at the Christmas celebration banquet of a local business. After the party, the owner gave me a check for $50.00. Today that isn't much, but fifty years ago, that $50.00 was big. Dot was trying to figure out how we could use it to make Christmas for our three children. I had something else in mind for it. We had a very strong discussion as to where the money would go. Dot won!

We spent four happy productive years with them and continue lifelong friendships with some of them in the years since.

Billy preaching

Billy preparing to perform a home wedding ceremony

IV.

SEASONS OF TRAGEDY AND TRIUMPH

"Oh, that we might know the Lord! Let us press on to know Him. He will respond to us as surely as the arrival of dawn or the coming of rain in early spring."

Hosea 6: 3 nlt

CHAPTER 14

SWEET WITH THE BITTER

MY EDUCATIONAL THIRST was rekindled, and I had the opportunity at Barton's Creek to enroll in the Master's degree program at Vanderbilt-Peabody University in Nashville. That was a commute of some seventy miles round trip for classes each day. By June of 1960, I had earned a Master of Arts degree and in June of 1961, a Specialist in Education degree. For someone with such a slow beginning, the odds of achieving such were extremely against having any academic success. The feeling was very good. I was freed from the trap of a lack of education.

I can't figure out how we ever made it financially, the salary was small, and I had to pay graduate school tuition—which was quite expensive—can't remember for sure, but you get the picture, and provide for two children with another on the way. It was a daunting task.

We had an old car—well over 10 years old—that I drove back and forth to Nashville every day. In addition I visited church families, held revivals, prepared sermons for two services on Sunday and one on Wednesday night, performed wedding ceremonies and conducted funerals. Then there were doctor's visits for the children, piano lessons, groceries to get, and errands to run, plus the normal activities necessary to keep the family functioning.

I loved Barton's Creek but was consumed with moving to a larger church. Before that happened, another of my dreams came true.

I'd always wanted to coach football and I was offered a position coaching football at the Mt. Juliet High School, a 20 minute drive from our house. I would also be a guidance counselor on the faculty there. Now I would have a teacher's salary in addition to my church salary. Our living conditions improved considerably. We even got a better car. One of the church members was a Ford car dealer. One day he said to me, "Pastor, you need a new car. I'll make you a special deal and help arrange financing for you." He did and now things were looking even better than ever.

ON SEPTEMBER 6, 1961, our third child, Jan, was born. Between teaching and coaching football at Mount Juliet High School and pastoring the Barton's Creek Baptist Church in Lebanon, life was full and challenging.

One Sunday in 1962, a pastor search committee from Eastwood Baptist Church in Bowling Green, Kentucky, showed up in the morning worship Service. Bowling Green was a thriving college town. The church called me to be their pastor. The congregation grew to over 500 members while we were there and our family was blessed with a strong, supportive group of friends. We were there for four years.

My next step was founding an evangelistic organization in 1966 to preach at revival meetings in local churches. I also bought a farm in nearby Scottsville, Kentucky, with money for the down payment borrowed from my mother. With our three children, we moved to Portland and I set out to preach evangelistic crusades, sometimes called revival meetings. After a while, though, I became weary of traveling and being away from my family for a week at a time. My being away nearly all the time was pulling me down. That was 1966.

The day after Christmas In 1967, our family and our dog loaded up and went to Camp Hill, Pennsylvania, to minister in a "pioneer" mission church.

By then, Terry was in the ninth grade, Al in the fourth, and Jan in the first. The whole family was adjusting to life there, everybody except me! I tried my hardest, but I simply could not find the groove to fit in.

Now, you can imagine, after all this moving around, that Dot was a bit frayed and on edge. I plumbed the depths of my soul for an answer for what to do. I was at the proverbial wit's end.

So, in July of 1968, because I had completed the work and received a Specialist in Education degree from Vanderbilt-Peabody University, I was offered a position with a government funded innovative counseling program called Reachigh. The goal was to set up counseling programs in high schools to work with teenagers. The program was based at Hendersonville High School but included high schools throughout the area. The family moved to Hendersonville, Tennessee

I promised Dot that we would not move the children again.

Along with this work, I pastored New Hope Baptist Church about 5 miles outside of Hendersonville, Tennessee. I did that for nine years preaching and pastoring, setting a record for my longevity.

Everybody quickly settled into life in that community. Dot was a counselor at nearby White House High School. The children, as usual, made friends and became involved in activities quickly, and I, along with counseling and pastoring, decided to pursue more education.

I enrolled in Luther Rice Seminary and subsequently received my Th.D. (Doctor of Theology) degree.

ON A SUNDAY MORNING in March, 1978, my wife I were on our way home from Church. We were waiting for the street light to turn green when a friend frantically hailed us down yelling "Hurry, hurry, your house is on fire."

Of course, we broke every speed limit getting to our house at 109 Jackstaff Drive in Hendersonville. Our front yard was filled with fire engines, police cars, ambulances, neighbors. Our house was indeed burning! Our home was going up in flames!

There was no way to save it or the possessions that had become precious to us over our 26 years of marriage (at the time) and raising a family of three. We had lived there for ten years, a record for us. Much living had gone on within those walls.

Terry had graduated from Belmont College, was teaching at Nannie Berry Elementary School in Hendersonville.

She had just been married to Randy Darnell in December of the year before. Her wedding dress and veil still were hanging in the bedroom that had been hers—ruined with smoke but not reduced to ashes.

Al was a student at the University of Tennessee in Knoxville, Tennessee. Many of his clothes were with him, but his room had been full of the memorabilia that boys collect who are active and good at sports. All of those trophies were lost!

Jan was still at home, a junior at Hendersonville High School. The fire had started in her bedroom from an electric blanket that shorted out at the outlet and filled the house with smoke. This had produced a flash fire with a temperature that melted and destroyed everything that the fire didn't get. Dot was a collector and every bit of the things she held dear—including an antique spool bed which had belonged to Jan's grandmother were gone.

Since Terry and Randy were newly married, much of her things were with her. However, her wedding dress still hung in her room—veil and all. Since the door was closed to her room, the dress survived, but no longer the champagne color it had been. It was browned from the smoke and heat.

We stood there and watched as the reality soaked in that we had nothing left—except the clothes on our back. Not even a toothbrush. None of the things we considered essential for making it through the day—and night! Not even a pillow on which to lay our heads—and no bed on which to lay the pillow.

There are a few times in life when a person is allowed to see what is important and what is not! When people come face to face with finding what they are made of. This was definitely one of those times. My family and I stood firmly against the shock we experienced. We picked ourselves up and began to gather any pieces we could find and put them back together again. We shed a few tears, shook ourselves, and began to dig into the ashes to see what could be salvaged. The challenge was to find out if what the Bible spoke of was true: could there really be an exchange of "ashes for beauty"? Could something really wonderful come from this devastating experience?

We quickly found that life does not consist of the things you possess. It is made up of people, of relationships. Every member of our family was alive and well—and determined. Not only that, we found how special friends are, how wonderful it was to have neighbors, how exciting it was to hear from many whom we did not even know. They rallied around to help, to support, to become involved in the recovery process in ways that showed us that the important aspects of our lives had not even been touched by the fire at all—not even singed! We were blessed beyond measure by the community in which we lived and by the unbreakable bond of love that united us more closely than ever.

Within a few weeks, the house was rebuilt, necessary furniture replaced—even a few pieces were salvaged and could be refinished. One piece we stained to cover the burn marks and it graces our home today.

Everybody got a new wardrobe—scant at best—but fresh and untouched by smoke and water damage. And the most important of all we discovered a better way of thinking—a new attitude—an appreciation for life itself and for the things that had brought peace and joy!

Even some of the irreplaceable things, such as pictures of our children's growing up years, which were lost, came floating back as those people to whom we had given pictures through the years began to return them to us. It was the boomerang theory that the Bible speaks of—what we had given away would come right back to us!

"We are merely moving shadows, and all our busy rushing ends in nothing. We heap up wealth, not knowing who will spend it. And so, Lord, where do I put my hope: My only hope is in You."

Psalm 39: 6-7 niv

CHAPTER 15

PRELUDE TO TRAGEDY AND TRIUMPH

IT WOULD SEEM that a fulltime job at the school and pastoring a church would be enough, and it was, but a golf course was being built nearby and there was a tract of land between there and a private lake called Willow Lake. I could visualize a community of attractive, appealing homes there that would sell like hotcakes. The land wasn't for sale, but a friend of mine knew the owner and made arrangements for me to talk with him. He sold me the property and it seemed this was meant to be. In a little while, I was developing the property and building houses and having good success in selling them.

I began to buy more land and develop it into subdivisions. This venture was crowned with success and led me into the best financial situation I had ever had. I liked it! The economy was open to the housing market and a building boom was at hand. I was immediately caught up in the process. It was exciting and rewarding. It gave life to that pull I had all my life to make money. Without realizing it, in my mind, I had equated having wealth with being somebody, with being successful in this life. This belief had laid dormant for a while and was strongly revived and brought to life by the rewards of this endeavor.

I found myself caught up in it. Even though I was still in the pastorate and high school counseling business. I now had three jobs. They consumed all my energy. Making money playing with land and real estate provided a thrill for me which was something like being on a roller coaster—up and down with each rise and dip more exciting than the last one!

After Willow Lake, it was a short step to developing a 50 lot subdivision in Hendersonville called Ridgecrest.

YOU MAY RECALL my earlier remarks about being fascinated by the political leaders in our county when my Dad was deputy sheriff. In 1972 I ran a political race for superintendent of schools in Sumner County.

It was one of the most challenging experiences I ever had. I was up at 5:00 a.m.—standing on the street corner handing out brochures to people going to work—waving a sign at those in cars. All day I was putting up campaign signs, in an out of restaurants, meeting people whenever and wherever I could. At night I was attending every event in every community in the county, trying to get votes, making speeches, talking to groups, being at factory gates as workers arrived or left work—shaking hand, shaking hands, shaking hands. I was up early and home late for 5 months.

The race was heated, but the political powers turned out to be too much for me to overcome. I lost the race by 500 votes.

That night I felt that the world had dropped from under me. I was so sure of a win. The next morning I walked into a restaurant for breakfast. A real estate broker motioned me to his table and said: "Sit down, Billy. Man, you're set to do real estate now. You've been months getting your name out there. You've met lots of people. Now take all that and go into real estate. No time to lick your wounds! Come on! Let's go look at this property right now."

So I did, and soon resigned my school position to devote full time to the buying and developing business. The boom was on, and so was I.

The next year I met Arlis Roberts who told me about their need for someone to locate motel sites for Days Inns, the largest budget motel chain in America, a chain of motels that now numbers into the hundreds of motels and hotels throughout the United States. He introduced me to Bob Dollar, the developer of building and franchise operations for the Days Inn chain. Since I seemed to have a keen insight into buying property, Bob enlisted me to locate and purchase sites for new inns. Bob and I became close friends. We both had attended Southern Seminary and pastored Southern Baptist Churches.

I was living life in the fast lane—and loving it!

I also began to trade in commodities, not only a high risk money-making venture but something that was exhilarating for me—for a while, that is. Commodity trading is a high loss-high win game in business. For a former school teacher, who was used to earning less than $11,000 a year, it was an exciting arena, where a person sometimes could make or lose $25,000 a day! Commodity trading soon came to occupy all of my thoughts and effort. It was addictive like hard drugs or heavy gambling where a person ends up virtually owing his soul to the mob, and perhaps also to the devil.

I had developed a system for trading thirty-year Treasury Bonds, and expended huge amounts of energy and countless hours perfecting my system. On paper it proved correct 85 percent of the time. Those in that type of trading are fully aware that if a system is right only 50 percent of the time, it will make a trader fabulously rich. Since my percentage was 85, surely I was going to become enormously wealthy.

During this time span, on a get-away weekend with my wife to Atlanta, I sat across the table from her and told her that I was well on my way to becoming a millionaire.

Sinking rapidly into the trap of greed. I was feeding on a diet of making money and all that goes with that. I was experiencing the feeling of success and importance that goes with accumulating riches. It was heady and I was losing myself in it!

I was about to learn tough-as-nails lessons, There were two factors that insidiously controlled a person indulging in the system, fear and greed. My system was by a long shot the best I had ever seen, and I had seen plenty of them. What's the problem? I kept asking myself. Man, you ought to have become a millionaire several times over. By every indication, I should have been way ahead instead of way behind. It hit me like the proverbial ton of bricks: I could neither control my fear nor my greed.

In high-risk undertakings, regardless of the so-called system, fear will gnaw away at your psyche. Then you will become terrified that somehow you are going to lose. When one is habitually fearful of losing, in most cases... he does exactly that—lose. So, with any compulsion, a person frantically searches for emotional props to keep him going. It is so insidious that your manic desperation causes you to grasp for straws instead of solid mainstays.

As my wealth grew, and the life style associated with it, I began to drink—alcohol—booze! The years from the time of our wedding in 1952 until 1973 were filled with so much activity: building a family, going to school for an education, entering the ministry, coaching, real estate, I never had a thought about drinking. There were occasions I was offered a beer, and I'd just ask for a Diet Coke. But in 1973 when I started becoming very successful—making a lot of money, which had insidiously become my measuring stick for success- my thinking began to change. When you have been making $11,000 a year as on teacher's salary—and that was a good salary for teachers since I was being paid for 10 years' experience counting my military time, plus 2 advanced degrees.

One night in Atlanta, having just closed a big real estate deal, I was having dinner with a good friend of mine, Randall Green. Randall said, "DeVasher, you need to celebrate tonight with a good glass of wine." I said "Ok. I'm ready to celebrate, but I'll have a diet coke." He ordered a glass of wine and I ordered the coke. From that point, I'm not sure what happened. He kept saying, "Bill, you ought to have a glass of wine and really get relaxed." I don't understand and I certainly can't explain it but for some unknown reason, Randall said: "Let me order you a glass of wine and I said 'what the heck'.

He ordered it and I drank it and we continued to drink into the night.

That one drink started a drinking habit that led into 18 years of drinking, a habit that was bordering on an addiction, into a trap of dependence, deceit, and hatred for myself.

When a person is on the road, too, it often has an adverse effect on him. Bored and with nothing to do at night, I also dropped in on bars to drink with friends (at least I thought they were my friends) a habit I had not indulged in for years. I hid it from my family and the congregation—at least I thought I was hiding it. I was not proud of myself but I convinced myself I could handle it. All people who drink think they can handle it—not realizing what they are dealing with—a powerful drug just waiting to enslave them, to trap them in the downward spiral to loss of control of their lives, and at one time, I was dangerously close to becoming an alcoholic. This trap was tightening its hold on me.

I started imbibing booze as though I were a fish in water, and also became involved in other activities of which I was not proud. Since God had guided me all of those years, and I had once invested my life in Him, how could I have turned in this perilous direction?

During those drinking days, I simply had to stop off at a lounge for the "happy hour", which usually ended up being the "unhappy hour". Like most seemingly respectable people who habitually drink, they live in denial, refusing to believe they have a drinking problem or are dependent on booze. I yearned for what I thought was relaxing and refreshing. After all, it was only a few drinks. Soon my "few drinks" were transformed into many. Believe it or not, when I was in town, I always ended up at home. Why I never had a serious car wreck or

DUI I will never understand except for the fact that someone was watching over me.

Through all of this, I was still in the real estate business—developing land and building. In 1973, I developed Parkwood Villa, a 168 unit apartment building.

I am not sure that what subsequently happened was a direct punishment for my hypocritical behavior, but it gave me cause for profound introspection about my spiritual life.

In 1974 the bottom fell out of all my enterprises. I lost every cent I had gained in real estate and commodities. By the end of the year I was completely broke. Why do I write candidly about all my ups and downs? So you might profit from my successes and failures. If it seems you are down, make up your mind to never be out. The key is resiliency. Pick yourself up and get back in the race. Our God is a God of second chances. He is able and willing to help, to guide, to give whosoever is willing the opportunity to do it over—and to do it right this time.

In 1976, I decided to run for county superintendent of schools for the second time. I barely lost this time. I plunged back into real estate deals. I was up and down. Lose a few. Win a few. The taste of bittersweet was in my mouth.

Nineteen seventy-seven was a mixture of good and bad. I developed another subdivision, Cragfront at Castalian Springs. After nine years, I resigned as pastor of New Hope Baptist Church. It was my decision, hopefully from the Lord, not theirs. In fact, I could have stayed on. They were kind, loving believers who put up with me with love and patience and without undue complaints. Some Church's favorite pastime is criticizing and vocally crucifying their pastor. That was not true of the New Hope folks. We began attending the Hendersonville Chapel.

Dot's sister's husband was killed in a car crash, and that set all of us back emotionally. Terry, our oldest daughter, married Randy Darnell in December of that year.

It was during this time span, our house burned.

One of my most eventful trips was to Chicago where I once again engaged in trading commodities. In addition, I kept on with my real estate business. We rebuilt a house. You have repeatedly heard that troubles come in bunches, and I suppose they do. Dot had to undergo surgery for breast cancer in 1979.

Six years after my business collapsed in 1974, it happened again. I then jumped into the spa business, traveling to Iowa and Chicago, where I opened spas and then sold them. Once more I picked myself up and started all over again, developing property on

Brick Church Pike in Nashville. Real-estate building and selling was in my blood. From 1983 to 1988 we opened up subdivisions: Oakwood Villa, Riverwood Drive, Lake Point Landing, Deer Point. My son Al, was working with me in all these enterprises. We also built and moved into a new house on Sumner Court in Hendersonville. It seemed as though we could heartily sing "Happy Days Are Here Again"… but…

"Listen to me—you whom I have upheld since you were conceived, and have carried since your birth. Even to your old age and gray hairs. I AM HE. I AM HE who will sustain you."

Isaiah 46:3-4

CHAPTER 16

MAXWELL

THE DOORBELL RANG. I was upstairs shaving. My wife went to the door. A Federal agent stood there with a notice for me to appear before Judge John Nixon in the Federal Court in Nashville, Tennessee, on August 19, 1990, for sentencing to federal prison. This notice came at the end of a two year investigation by the FBI. They had spent two years examining every file where I had sold townhouses in two multiple family developments.

The first development was Lakepoint—78 units. The second was Deer Point—112 units.

My attorney, Vince Wehby, had been negotiating with the FBI on my behalf well over a year. I was being charged with a HUD (Housing Urban Development) violation. Their findings showed that I had paid some down payments for people who were buying houses. We had been advertising our program for over two years so we had nothing to hide. The title companies, mortgage companies, FHA, the lenders—all knew of our program and were all working with us.

In one of the last meetings with my attorney, I told him I wanted to go to court and prove I had done nothing wrong—I argued that I had done nothing that the lending agencies did not know about. The down payments came from my pocket. None of it came from the government He told me that anytime the FBI worked on a case two to two and a half years, there would be a charge of a crime.

I laughed and said: "Vince, I'm no criminal—never been arrested in my life."

My lawyer told me that 98% of those who were indicted by the government and went to court lost the case.

I continued to be defensive: "But I'm not guilty."

He replied: "Billy it's white collar crime. In your mind you feel as if you were helping people and not guilty of any crime, but this is the government you're going up against and you can't win."

I took their plea bargain deal.

And on the morning of August 19, 1990, I stood before Judge John Nixon in Federal Court and received a sentence of 6 years to be served in federal prison.

The next day, the newspaper told the story. Headlines! As I read the paper, I became very angry, very intimated, very depressed. I thought: I haven't hurt anyone, haven't cheated anyone. I was the one carrying the down payment.

It became humiliating, embarrassing for me. We had lived in Hendersonville for 25 years. I had been a high school teacher and counselor, pastor of a local church, a successful business man. My wife at the time was a counselor at the local high school. My children were achieving academically and athletically. No one had ever been charged with anything or arrested. Here I was, having served in two wars. It was about all I could bear. The feeling was intense.

Day by day the anger increased and there was no peace in my life. My wife, with Christian faith a lot stronger than mine, assured me, we were going to get through it.

On October 1, 1990, Dot and I left our home in Hendersonville at 4:30 in the morning. Billy DeVasher, officially on the books as "a felon" and a "criminal" was driving to his new home, 305 miles away in the federal prison camp in Montgomery, Alabama, located on the Maxwell Air Force Base. On the way out of town. we passed Deer Point, one of the two developments I had built and had worked 12 to 15 hours a day doing so, and now I was going to prison for it.

I had orders to report before five o'clock so we had time for a leisurely trip, a good breakfast, and a lot of conversation all the way. We talked about our lives, the ways in which we had been blessed, the way life would be now—changes and what we would need to do in order to survive this. We dreamed of how it would be when it was all over. Because of our belief in the providence, grace, and forgiveness of the Jesus Christ, of our trust in His redemptive love and His promises of restoration, we were not downbeat or discouraged. That would come later with the separation and realities of prison life. All in all, it was a great but sad day! It was both painful and good to get on with this difficult thing we faced.

We had a leisurely trip and arrived at Maxwell Federal Prison at 4:00 in the afternoon, an hour before check-in deadline. My wife let me out at the entrance of this minimum security prison and waited and watched until she could no longer see me and knew that I would not be returning that day through that door.

I went into the registration center and was met by a guard who escorted me to where I was to report. He then took me to a holding area until someone came for me from the building I would live in.

The holding area also served as a visitation room. As I was sitting there, one of the inmates came over to talk to me. He said, "You're just coming in. Let me tell you about this place. It's not a good place to be. It's going to be rough."

I wasn't feeling too friendly. My reply was: "Let me tell you something, son." (I called him son because I was 62 and he was 25.) "I've been in two wars. I was a Marine on Fox Hill at the Chosin Reservoir in North Korea. Compared to that, this will be like a boy scout camp."

He went on his way; and I determined at that moment that I would get tough and be tough. I would do what I had to do to make it.

That dismal day was an all-time low for me. When I walked into that facility, I was mad. As the days passed, I withdrew into myself, despising myself, my surroundings, and the people I felt responsible for my incarceration.

One of the initial experiences there was an orientation into the cold, hard realities of life in prison. He emphasized that one of the worst aspects of life there was adjusting to the fact that we had lost our freedom. Yes, I had realized that the day I walked in, although Maxwell was a minimum security prison and there were no walls to hem you in and no bars to clang shut behind, there was the reality of definite limits and you knew you could not exceed those limits without repercussions. You were not free! You were in a trap—a trap from which you could not escape.

The warden also indicated that some of us would find ourselves in a state of depressed remorse, similar to mourning a death in the family or the loss of a loved one by separation or divorce. Most of the men would pass the hours grieving over the loss of their freedom.

It seemed the last time I had fully expressed concern about freedom was when I fought with the Marines for the South Koreans. I had volunteered for combat—wasn't drafted. That freedom for which I personally fought had now been snatched from my grasp. Everything I did was regimented and controlled. I couldn't go to Rivergate Mall and walk, stop at a restaurant for a meal, drop by Walgreen's Drug Store or drive out for a cone of Baskin Robbins ice cream. I couldn't even pick up the phone whenever I wanted and call a friend or business associate—or even my wife until a specified time of the day or night—and then there was a time limit. I was no longer free!

Everybody was assigned a job to do. You were paid for doing it. The money went into an account which we could use at the commissary. Our pay was eleven cents an hour!

The job I was assigned to was on the Maxwell Air Force Base. The officer there in charge of inmates assigned me to an office to answer the telephone. I thought there would probably be a few calls coming in. I was wrong. It didn't take long to see there were calls coming in from all over the world. I was supposed to take the calls and direct them to the person requested. A lot of time you would be talking to high ranking officers in another part of the world. My hearing was impaired—and still is. One day a call came in from a Colonel in Germany who engaged me in a conversation, saying: "You sound like a Southerner. Where are you from?"

"Tennessee."

"I'm from Alabama," he said."

I answered, "Roll Tide,"

He replied, "You're a fan. That's great. What's your position there?"

"I'm an inmate."

"You're what?"

"I'm doing time here."

"How could you be and doing the job you're doing?"

I wanted to tell him that I'm a Marine and Marines can do any job—but I didn't. I just put him through to his party.

After a few days I began to find the job stressful because of my lack of hearing. I had to be constantly on the alert, being careful not to make a mistake, wondering about doing all this for 11 cents an hour. One day the Air Force Sergeant was standing behind me and heard me ask the caller to repeat the name of the person with whom he wanted to speak. He immediately called a van and had me picked up to go back to the Camp. Because of my hearing, I wasn't what they needed.

It was January 18, my birthday, and I was being fired! That didn't do a whole lot to add to my celebration that day.

However, it turned out to be a blessing! I got a job in food service—that's the cafeteria where all the food was—and one thing about prison was that the food was plentiful and great. We wore white uniforms instead of the green other prisoners wore and the atmosphere was better than any place else on the grounds.

EVEN SO, THE feelings of anger and frustration that I had went on until Thanksgiving. I was not a very happy camper. Thanksgiving was one of my favorite times of the year. I had a wonderful family and home and here I was cut off from them.

To make my feelings worse, I got a letter that day from my oldest daughter. She was one of the apples of my eye. There were two other children just as wonderful to me, her brother and sister. She was born when I was in the Marine Corps and living on a Sergeant's pay. We didn't have a lot of money for luxuries but she had brought love into my life that was worth all the luxuries in the world. She had lived a life I was so proud of my children and our family.

At mail call that day, I got her letter. I walked over to a llttle lake with benches around it. No one was there but me. In the letter, she told me how proud she was of me, how courageous I had been and that she knew I would make it. She told me how much she loved me and what a good father I had been for her.

I finished reading and then I lost it. I began to cry, to weep. Until that time, I had not shed a tear. It made me realize that, no matter how bad it might be, how angry and depressed I might be, that I still had my family and that was the greatest thing in the world. My real hurt was being separated from those who loved me most.

God always has a way, out of the goodness of His love, to make things better.

IT WAS THANKSGIVING Eve. All day, I thought about Thanksgiving at home—the big dinners, the whole family together, plenty to eat, talk, visit, watch football into the night. My thinking threw me into a mood that was darker and darker. My desire to be home was overwhelming. I could think of nothing else, and as time went on it became all consuming, leading me into a depression like I had never experienced before. Except for the time I was in the Marine Corps, I had never missed a Thanksgiving Day celebration with my family. The thought of doing it now was unacceptable.

The fact that we had had a big meal that evening didn't help. All that was bearing on my mind. When the meal was finished, it was beginning to get dark. I went out to River Road to walk, River Road ran beside the Alabama River and I walked to the far end of it. No one else was out. Everybody had gone back to their bunks. It was a beautiful night—not cold at all down in Alabama, but honestly, the beautiful night and big dinner meant nothing to me because my life was filled with anger and hate and a lot of frustration causing me to be very depressed.

I was looking at the ten foot fence that separated the road from the river. I was so beside myself that I said to myself: "I'm going to climb the fence and I'm going to jump in the river." I just couldn't seem to bear the thoughts that possessed me—that I had messed up my life so bad. I said to myself—I can end all this right here, right now. I had hit bottom!

I had been a believer in Jesus Christ for many years, had grown up in the Methodist Church in the town where we lived. For many years, I had believed in God and even taught others about Him, but I stood there in complete desperation. I don't have the words to describe how I felt. The more I reflected, the worse it became. All of my negative feelings eating away at me, making me sick emotionally, physically, and spiritually. I was being dragged downward into a morass of contemptible thoughts and words.

In my despair, I lifted my hands toward Heaven and thought: How did I ever get so far from God?

When I lifted my hands, I said a very simple prayer—I just cried out to Him with the same cry I had heard on the battlefield, the same cry in the hospital room, the same cry in the federal court room. I cried, "Dear God, please help me.!"

With my conviction and imprisonment I had been stripped bare of all my supposed smartness and slickness. My capitalistic savvy, my independent arrogance. I had become a modern-day Job. Now I was in a position where God could speak to me and be heard. I was completely helpless. You name the adjective: weak, incompetent, ineffective, powerless, bungling. Oh, how I had prided myself on being an activist, proud, tough. I had been the guy who could make the deal. I had been the doer with accomplishments to prove it. I previously had connections, but I had distanced myself from the ultimate connection—God through Jesus Christ. I wasn't even at the end of my rope, for all the rope was gone!

Then I heard God speak. "Back off, Billy! You're crowding me."

I jumped three steps backward and stood stock still, my arms outstretched, my mouth open but silent as a lamb.

He continued to lay it out before me: "Listen to me! Thanksgiving is not the most important thing in your life. I AM! I am the most important thing in your life. There will be other Thanksgivings. You will share them with your family, but tonight I am here, and I am here for you, even as I always have been."

Only moments before I foolishly felt I had no one to turn to, in spite of my education, in spite of my ministry in churches, in spite of the spiritual nurture I had received. Now I realized once again that the Master of the universe was there with me and for me the true and living God was with me. In spite of all my mistakes, my failures, He was there for me! His work on the cross had sent my mistakes, my sins as far from me as the east is from the west. My faults were buried in the deepest of seas! I was forgiven, accepted, made whole! All because of his grace and mercy!

With my arms outstretched, I immediately felt the presence, the power, the love of God come into my life as I had never known before. It seemed that His Spirit and love washed over me like a refreshing rain and the anger, the frustration, the depression drained away.

I felt like a new man. I was a new man! All of my gloom evaporated into thin air. I started smiling for the first time in months. The smile turned into laughter and I began to rejoice and praise my God.

In all of my life I had never experienced such awe and wonder. The freedom I had lost was replaced with an unbelievable, supernatural freedom.

As I stood there on that road, I was reminded of Jesus' words: "You shall know the truth and the truth shall set you free." Jesus said, "I am the Way, the Truth, and the Life." He, the Truth, set me free that night. All of my pent-up anger, frustration, and hate drained from me like brackish oil from a car. All of the bad dissipated, and the overflowing love of Jesus suffused my life. As God filled me with Himself, there was no room for any of the negatives. Love, forgiveness, freedom, joy! These feelings flowed into me—but it was more than feelings! It was reality!

IT WAS QUITE a while before I got back to my cubicle, my bunk. I made it just in time to be counted. There was a count seven times a day. Every inmate had to be in his assigned place and be counted. This was the last count. It was 9 o'clock! I was there!

A lot of nights I couldn't sleep. This night, I didn't even want to sleep. I kept thinking about what had happened to me. A few hours earlier, I had hate, now I had love; I had frustration, anger, now I had peace. I felt I was at peace with all men. God had done a miracle in my life beyond what I could ever imagine. And He had done it in an instant. I had been a certified counselor with graduate degrees to prove it—plus 20 years' experience in pastoral counseling. I knew how much time work and effort would be involved in bringing about a change like the one that had taken place in me. I knew God had worked a miracle in my life!

And the wonder of it all is that the phenomenal experience of that night has never departed from me!

Toward morning, I fell off to sleep for a couple of hours. Then morning came: Thanksgivings Day! We had no duties—it was a holiday—and we had phone privileges that started at 9 o'clock. I went back to walk on River Road for a couple of hours waiting for the time I could call my wife. I was thinking of all the Thanksgivings I'd experienced with my family, going hunting with my Dad, all the big dinners. As I thought, I did not feel lonely or separated or hurt or angry. All that was gone. I felt whole, like I was a new person and I remembered the Scripture which said that "old things are passed away. Behold all things have become new."

When I called my wife, I was jubilant. What Billy Graham had said was true, I had "a spring in my step, a smile on my face, and a thrill in my heart."

I told my wife what a great Thanksgiving Day it was going to be. I suppose she thought I would be very sad and lonely because I wouldn't be home. I told her something wonderful had happened to me and I was o.k. I was really more than o.k. When she came to visit the next day, I would explain it all to her.

Everything changed! My job working in the mess hall for two to three hours a day left the rest of the day with free time for me. We had a library where I went each day, but most of my free time was spent walking on River Road. I averaged 20 miles a day walking—sometimes walking 25. I soon acquired a reputation as "the guy who walked". I was content with walking and thanking God for what he'd done for me and with looking forward to the time when I would be going home.

IT DIDN'T SEEM that long until I had my first meeting with the parole board. My wife drove down and they allowed her to come to the hearing. We met. Everything was fine. The only problem was they released no one with as little time served as I had served—percentage wise.

A few months went by and I met again with the review board—three guys I really liked: the chaplain, the assistant warden, and a social worker. They determined that I could be released because I had a home to go to, a family, and a job. They said that my situation being what it was "You've been a model prisoner here so for the next five years you won't have to stay here. You'll be on parole; you can go on with your life—with no history of drugs, behavior problems or anything like that, you will be released in 2 to 3 months."

It was hard to describe but the next 3 months was a joyful time. I began to pray while I walked on River Road, read my Bible more, my relationship with the Lord grew. He was now so real to me. To think that a few short weeks ago, I thought He had left me for I didn't know where He was. Those few months passed fast.

When I look back over that year, I think what it had meant to me. Physically, I had lost a lot of unwanted weight. I had gotten in excellent shape walking River Road and in the weight room. Spiritually God had become very real to me. My walk with Him was now wonderful! The time I spent there could very well turn out to be the best year of my life!

Billy and Dot at Maxwell

"...No longer will I call you slaves, for the slave does not know what his master is doing; but I have called you friends....."

John 15: 15 niv

CHAPTER 17

WALKING ON

THE WALKING AND running tracks at Maxwell Prison Camp surrounded the prison compound. The track was behind the golf course separated by a fence. It ran between two lakes and onto the golf course. We could walk on the road, but going onto the golf course was forbidden.

I worked at Maxwell Air Force Base. Every morning, bright, or even gloomy, and early, about 600 inmates would leave the prison camp to go to work. After a full day's work on the base, we would return to the camp for evening chow and rest, and then the routine would resume as usual the following morning.

Shortly after Thanksgiving at Maxwell, I was assigned to the prison mess hall. The crew there was made up of unexpected persons: the ex-governor of a nearby state, a prominent banking mogul, a CPA, a doctor who had run a thriving medical center, a casino owner, an airplane pilot, and others. They were there for various and sundry reasons, such as business fraud, forgery, counterfeiting, and money laundering. Some were there because of drug trafficking. One was a big-time drug lord from a Latin American country.

My job at the mess hall was waiting tables, cleaning off tables and scrubbing the floors until the inspector could eat off them if he so chose. They had to be scrubbed after every meal.

The inmates engaged in all sorts of tasks on the base. Though it was against the rules to swing a golf club or pick up a ball, many manicured the golf course. Others labored on the grounds, in the commissary, the supply house, in the maintenance department, the offices, the hospital. Fortunately, the work was not unpleasant, and the civilian and military people with whom we worked were usually friendly and decent toward you. Naturally, every once in a while an authority figure would assert himself and remind you of his power over you. I discovered that being in prison or the military is like anywhere else. Most of the time, if you want to hit if off with people, you can get along.

My lifelong belief about people has been that most of them try to do the best they can in the situation they're in. Some succeed better than others. At Maxwell, a person lived pretty much to himself. You never asked anybody what he was there for. There were a lot of dark secrets and nobody trusted anybody else. One man told he hated the guards and never looked at them. It was a world of every man out for himself.

THE FIRE ALARM often went off in the middle of the night—around 2 o'clock in the morning or so. Everyone had to dress hurriedly and get out of the building ASAP—regardless of the weather.

In the winter months, we stood outside—in the cold or rain—until the fire truck got there with the firemen in full attire. They rushed into the building to locate the fire and extinguish it. Ironically, we all knew there was no fire. Either an inmate—or sometimes a guard—had pulled the alarm. No one ever knew who.

On one occasion the alarm had gone off several nights in a row between one and three o'clock. This night as we were standing outside in the chilling rain, the Warden showed up accompanied by three guards. He got up on the steps. One of the guards handed him a bullhorn. It was easy to see—and hear—how upset he was!

With his commanding voice, his message came across clearly:

"There's an inmate here who is causing you to have to be out here in this cold freezing rain. I want you to know that if you are all dumb enough to allow this to continue—to let it go on—you deserve this and more ....so look forward to many more nights standing out here in the rain...."

He really got the attention he planned for. I never heard who was pulling the alarm or how it all happened. I just know that the fire drills came to an end. There was not another one during the time I was there!

AT MAXWELL, A person's former position or past achievements—good ones, that is—did not matter: you were a criminal, a convicted felon. You didn't have a name; you had a number. After a while, as I had become acquainted with a few of the others there, I suggested to an inmate: "Hey, guess what. They ought to close this place down."

Naturally, he asked why.

I wryly replied, "Because….nobody in this place is guilty of anything. Everybody says he's innocent. Nobody says he's done anything wrong."

CHRISTMAS WAS HARD there. Every inmate had a difficult time handling that season. Some men measured their time there by Christmases. I asked, "How long have you been here?" The answer would be: "Ten Christmases." or "two Christmases" or "four Christmases." After my first—and only — Christmas there, I could understand why.

On Christmas Day we worked until noon. Then we came back to the barracks. On our bunks was a gift in a plastic bag. I don't recall what it was—

something inconsequential—but it was a gift and I appreciated the thought. Some of the men there had never received a Christmas gift.

An attempt was made to make it a little special. Christmas carols were playing throughout the barracks and about 5 o'clock we had Christmas dinner. They tried to provide a traditional Christmas dinner, but nothing like the one we would have if we were home.

We ate well—all the time. Living conditions were close. Two men lived in what was called a cube. The cubes were separated by concrete block walls—about shoulder height. You could see over them. There were bunk beds and a small locker for each person. Combination locks were provided and everybody was careful to keep them locked—everybody but me. My lock lay on the shelf inside the locker. A few things were stolen, but even though I lived with people who were serving time for robbing banks, I found myself trusting them as I do everybody else.

One purpose my locker served was for the food I could bring home from the mess hall where I worked. I shared it with others. Meals were a big deal. Things ran smooth there—probably because the men were well fed. If you worked in food service, you wore white uniforms and were sort of a special breed. Some guys would get up at 2 o'clock in the morning to work in the bakery. A couple of mornings a week there served fresh cinnamon rolls and donuts. When they finished their baking and cleaned up, these guys were off the rest of the day.

A civilian was head of the food service, had been for about fifteen years. If anyone caused any trouble or failed to do his job or couldn't get along with others, he bounced them out of food service immediately. He took great pride in his work and wanted you to do the same.

The threat of an uprising surfaced once in the camp. The rumor was that a policy was being changed which some didn't like. The word was passed that soon there would be a prison riot. That evening I sat down at a table with a man who had been there a long time—to see if I could find out anything about the rumor. He was definite, "Look boys, there isn't going to be a riot. As long as they keep on filling these bellies full, there won't be a riot! And he was right—nothing happened and the good meals kept coming!

The punishment was that you were away from your family. When you had a family you loved—and who loved you—on a special day, the punishment was simply not being with them.

You could have visitors, and my wife wanted to come Christmas Day. She averaged driving the 306 miles from our driveway to Maxwell every other weekend but I said no. She needed to be with the family on this day—with things as normal as possible. She came the day after Christmas and we visited on Saturday and Sunday of that weekend until three o'clock in the afternoon when visitation was over. It wasn't anything like our usual Christmas celebration, but a time of unusual joy!

BEFORE I STARTED working in the dining hall, I stayed mostly to myself, but one day a couple of guys invited me to join them and several others in the Chapel. They wanted to initiate a prayer group. There were a lot of people and circumstances that needed prayer. I agreed and felt it was a good way to spend my time.

So, we started an around-the-clock, twenty-four-hour-a-day prayer chain. At night, you couldn't get out of your cube area unless you were going to the bathroom. That made it impossible to notify the next person who was to pray in the chain. That person needed to be wakened. When one moved out of his area (sometimes to another floor) he was in danger of getting in trouble. The guard walked through the barracks all night, but they soon learned what was going on and who was involved in this round the clock prayer chain so they would let it pass.

It was amazing how many lives were touched as a result of our prayer chain. Almost every night—right after the evening meal—we would meet and talk about who we needed to pray for on our watch. We started praying for the Warden of the prison, his staff, the guards. Strange thing, a few days before the prayer chain started, I hated the guards. That feeling melted away. We witnessed the power of God and although the chain was still going when I was released, I don't know how long it lasted after that, but that prison had never seen anything like what was happening. The guards were very supportive.

Since I had loads of free time in between meals, I was able to pray several hours a day. I assumed my prayer time while walking on River Road, averaging about 20 miles a day— sometimes jogging, mostly walking. I had already lost about forty pounds. I was going to Bible study almost every night, and soon our prayer group grew to 100 inmates, almost one-tenth of our population. In addition, a number of the staff members and guards were supportive. A surprising number of the seemingly hard-boiled guards were Christians or at least interested in the faith.

The group was knit together. One of the group leaders had a lot of leadership ability. He had managed a casino. He also had a lot of love for the guys. One day on his call to his wife, she said she could come that weekend for a visit. He told her he couldn't be available to see her on Friday night because he had a meeting with his boys in his prayer group. When he told me about that, I said: "Frank, you're out of your mind, you're telling me you're passing on seeing your wife to be with a group of inmates." It was that important to him.

Not only was I being changed but one by one the involved inmates were coming to Christ for the first time or either rededicating themselves to the Lord. Nothing else describes it but "awesome". All around us men were inquiring about how to receive Christ and to live for Him. They were hungering and thirsting for God and all He had to offer them: peace, consolation, serenity, and tranquility at heart, mind, and spirit.

Sometimes I felt as if I were in a monastery where prayer, meditation, contemplation, and spiritual discipline were the order of the day, instead of a prison. That was a blessing beyond expression.

MY LIFE HAD become a wonderful mystery to me! Here I was—supposed to be suffering as a result of my wrong doing—and instead, I was enjoying some of the happiest days of my whole life. I had been changed and the bonds that had chained me all of my life were being broken. I was set free. As the days passed, I became increasingly convinced that God Himself was behind my being there so He could alter the course of my life. It takes a miracle to get some folks out of prison. It took a miracle to get me into prison.

It helped that I met with a group of guys on Friday nights to study the AA Big Book. Some had been in the 12 step program for quite a while. Others of us had had problems with booze and for various reasons has not been able to quit. Before going to prison, my drinking had become a serious problem with me. I had tried on many occasions to quit it. Sometimes I'd quit for a few days. Sometimes a few weeks or even sometimes a few months. I shared my story with the group. One of the group said, "Billy, you said in your sharing with us that you had never been a member of the AA 12 step program. A lot of us men are in this program for a lifetime in order to stay sober, so don't think it's going to get better. For a while, you may be all right. Then something will trigger it and you 'll be back where you were."

After my River Road experience with God, I have never had the desire to drink again, and there have been lots of ups and downs—many that could have triggered such a desire—but it's never happened. God set me free and I have been "free indeed" ever since.

Running from the will of God I had plunged myself into work. It was business every day and happy hour every evening. I had erected my own idols and they had taken up their position between God and me. Now that I was walking in the Spirit and had fellowship with Him, I was painfully aware of my previously wasted years. The "Hound of Heaven", as Francis Thompson referred to Him, had sniffed me out, tracked me down and drawn me back into the center of God's fold.

V.

A SEASON OF GRACE

"Anyone who belongs to Christ has become a new person. The old life is gone; a new life has begun! and all of this is a gift from God."
II Corinthians 5:17-18 nlt

CHAPTER 18

HOMECOMING

AFTER SERVING NINE months of a six year sentence I was released to go home. When I walked out of Maxwell Prison Camp, it seemed the sky was never bluer, the foliage was never greener. The hot July breeze, rather than oppressive, was never more invigorating. All of nature seemed to be celebrating with me.

No. They didn't give me a new suit of clothes and ten dollars, but they did bid me farewell as I left.

The bus ride from Montgomery to Nashville required all day and was a reminder of all the trips I had made while in the Marine Corps. Even the old Greyhound bus seemed to be a regal chariot. The motley group of people packed into that bus seemed to be either spiritual children of God or potential followers of Him.

A revitalized Billy DeVasher was leaving one world and returning to another. I was being released from a minimum security prison to a halfway house. This meant going home to my work and to my family every day and returning to the halfway house to sleep at night. After six months, I served out the remaining five years of my sentence at home but on probation.

A probation officer was assigned to me and I was expected to report to him on a regular basis. My officer was a special person and for five years, I reported to him every month. We would talk about what was going on and how I was doing.

In our first visit, he explained the procedure to

me. He never referred to me as an inmate. He called me by my first name, Billy, and he said, "You are going to get along very well. You have no history of drugs and no problem with keeping the rules so far. However, let me warn you that if you violate the rules of probation, you will immediately be sent back to prison to finish out the next five years of your sentence there—and they may send you to a lockdown prison instead of the minimum security place where you were. Just the other night I had to go into a bar and handcuff a man who was drunk and causing a lot of trouble, and send him back to prison. No alcohol, no drugs. Another time I went into a home where a person was abusing his wife. I had to do the same thing with him. Send him back."

"You cannot have a firearm in your possession or in your home. You cannot leave this area, especially the state without permission…"

He asked me what kind of job I was planning to

get. I told him I wasn't too interested in any job at the moment. When I looked back to what sent me to prison—building and selling townhomes—working at least fourteen hours every day—in sense the work that had sent me there, I was interested in a different kind of life.

The next monthly meeting we had, he said his supervisor had gotten with him because I didn't have a job yet. The supervisor wanted to come to my house the next month, came to my house, told me I had to have a job and begin paying restitution to the government in the way of money. He suggested that a job at Wal-Mart as a greeter would be good. My friend, Jim Burrow, suggested that I apply for my Social Security and pay them out of that—which seemed like a good idea—the government paying the government.

During the time when my family went on vacation, usually to Florida, I so badly wanted to go, and they wanted me to go with them, but I didn't. I probably could have but I was not going to take the risk.

At the end of the probation period, I told my probation officer that my wife and I would like to take him and his wife out to dinner. He said that was against the rules and I never saw him again. My probation was over! I was finally really free!

When I had walked out of the prison five years earlier, it was a relief—but the day that I was freed from probation, I felt the weight of the world fall from my shoulders.

It seemed I was not only transported by the bus, but by the Holy Spirit who carried me on a reminiscent tour of my entire life (which in itself sounds dreadfully tiring, but it wasn't to me!). People often claim that their entire lives pass in review when they are about to die. Mine passed through the back roads of my mind…and I was not only about to live! I already was vibrantly alive!

When this guy at Maxwell found out I was being released, he asked me how did I think the people in my community would receive me when I got home.

The reason he asked was that he was a deacon in his church back home and would soon be going home himself. He was apprehensive. How would it be? How would people look at him? How would he be received?

He had been an automobile dealer in that town and was sent to Maxwell because of some financing problems. He had been active in his church. His pastor sent his associate pastor to visit him one weekend. He knew both men well. This emissary told him that the pastor and the deacons is his church had talked about it and had come to the conclusion that it would be better for him to go to another church when he got home. That message hurt him deeply.

I told him I wasn't worried about how I would be received, that the Lord had forgiven me, that there were builders in the church doing the same thing I was , that the old saying that "the church is a hospital for sinners"—at least it should be—and that I, like Paul, was a chief sinner. Perhaps it would say more about them than about me if they refuse to receive me back. I had been forgiven and set free—and that was enough for me!

One of the first five people I visited when I got home was Dr. Glenn Weekley, the Pastor of my church. I walked in his study. He hugged me and said, "Billy, I'm really glad to see you. Sit down and tell me what's happened to you."

I told him of my encounter with the Lord and how my being in prison had become one of the best years of my life. He started laughing, and said "Billy, what you did was you took the stick that the devil was going to use on you and you beat him over the head with it…"

He continued: "Now I want to ask you to share your testimony with the church…"

Later, on Thanksgiving Eve when our church membership was gathered for thanksgiving dinner celebration, I did that.

I was received with open arms!

One of the men at the dinner that night invited Dot and me to eat with them at a local restaurant. While there, they introduced us to a weekend ministry called *Tres Dias* and invited us to participate in the three day weekend retreat with the Lord. We went and were tremendously blessed and became a part of this ministry for several years.

We found that some people never forgive. We found that most of God's people are endowed with the spirit of forgiveness and recognize that we're all in the same boat when it comes to having "fallen short of the glory of God". Most people know that it is only because of the perfection of the Lord Jesus Christ that any of us will have eternal life. It is only because of his willingness to take our place and pay the price for our redemption on the cross. I am eternally thankful for that!

"God can do anything, you know—far more than you could ever imagine or guess or request in your wildest dreams!"

Ephesians 3: 30 msg

CHAPTER 19

THE SILVER STAR

EARLY IN MAY, 2000, I was in my office working on a real estate deal. The phone rang. A very official-sounding voice told me it was a call from the headquarters of the Commandant of the United States Marine Corps in Washington, D.C.—a call for Billy DeVasher. Thus far it had been one of those days when everything that could go wrong had gone wrong. Now, I said to myself—the Marines are after me!

The caller verified who I was and explained that on Flag Day, June 14, 2000, the Marine Corps would be having a commemoration of the 50th anniversary of the end of the Korean War. There would be a reception at the Commandant's home followed by a parade. The President's Band would perform and a special ceremony would follow at which you, Billy DeVasher, will be awarded the Silver Star recognizing your service and bravery in action at the Chosin Reservoir in November, 1950, during the Korean War.

He said that if you and you wife can come, the Marine Corps will pay all your expenses. Two Marines will meet you on your arrival at the airport and be your escorts throughout your stay here. The Commandant himself will personally pin the Silver Star on you.

"Now let me ask you," he said. "Can you and your wife come?"

I quickly replied, "Captain, I think you have the wrong man."

He said, "You are Billy G. DeVasher?

I answered, "Yes, I am."

He asked, "And you were in the United States Marine Corps in Korea in 1950?

I affirmed that, "Yes, sir, I was."

He continued, "And you were on Fox Hill at the Chosin Reservoir in November of that year?"

It was a response spoken in shock, "Yes, sir, I was."

"No doubt about it then, I have your Silver Star and the situation accompanying it sitting right here on my desk."

Without hesitation, my next words were. "We'll be there!"

Those few days in the nation's capital were unreal, unbelievable. We were treated like royalty! We were guests at a ceremony at the Tomb of the Unknown soldiers at Arlington Cemetery celebrating Flag Day. We visited the grave of my wife's brother who was a retired Naval pilot when he died and was buried in Arlington Cemetery. We were honored that night with a reception which several hundred attended at the official home of the Commandant. This was the official location for honoring the recipients of the Silver Star and others Marine awards of honor. There was a parade ground larger than a football field and Marine Barracks for those assigned to special events. A trio of musicians played for the reception. Hor d'oerves were served along with cocktails. The Marine Band and special Rifle Team performed for the crowd.

Washington dignitaries attended including Senator Ted Kennedy and Senator John Warner, former Secretary of the Navy. Senator John Kerry, who is presently Secretary of State participated in the evening. One outstanding guest for me was Sergeant Major John Henry who was my Platoon leader at the Chosin Reservoir on Fox Hill—he was responsible for saving my life.

The President's Band was spectacular in its performance, as was the Marine Rifle Team whose exhibition was flawless and unbelievable. They were all there for one reason and that for me was the thing of which dreams are made when I was escorted to the center of the parade ground and was decorated with the Silver Star.

The Master of Ceremonies read the citation:

"The President of the United States takes pleasure in presenting the SILVER STAR MEDAL to Billy DeVasher for service as set forth in the following:

For conspicuous gallantry and intrepidity in action in connection with operations against the enemy while serving as Machine Gun Squad Leader, Company F, 2nd Battalion, 7th Marines, 1st Marine Division in Korea, from 26 November to 2 December, 1950. The Company was tasked with securing the Toktong Pass and providing security along the road between Hagari and Yudamni. Over the course of five days and six nights of bitter cold sub-zero weather, Corporal DeVasher displayed outstanding courage and initiative in the performance of his duties. During the night of 26 November, the company was repeatedly attacked by a large enemy force of Chinese Army soldiers. Exposing himself, without regard for his personal safety, to devastating enemy automatic weapons, hand grenades, and small arms fire, he fearlessly moved through the position during the attacks to encourage his men and direct their fire. When the enemy reached within yards of his positions, Corporal DeVasher courageously remained in an exposed position to beat them back, employing hand grenades, and his rifle with telling effect. Throughout the night-long attack, he refused to seek safety for himself, continuing to direct the fire of his gun and routing the enemy with heavy losses. On one occasion, he provided flank security and saved the life of a fellow Marine during actions to capture an enemy sniper located in front of their defensive position. By his extraordinary heroism in the face of extreme danger, Corporal DeVasher reflected great credit upon himself and upheld the highest traditions of the Marine Corps and the United States Naval Service." It is signed by the Secretary of the Navy for the President.

What was so special about the event was that I had never been honored the way I was that night. It seemed it was all about me. I had never thought (and did not think it that night) that I was important enough to be recognized in such a way, but the Commandant assured me I was by telling me (after he pinned the Silver Star on) that I had been a good Marine and that he was promoting me to my next rank of Gunney Sergeant. (I had been promoted to

Staff Sergeant while on recruiting duty in Nashville after my combat time in Korea.)

The promotion was very significant. A couple of years ago I was at a Marine Corps reunion where a writer for the Marine Cops magazine, "The Leatherneck", was sitting at my table. He told me who he was and I said, "I think I have a story for you. Check this out, because I believe I have set a record in the Marine Corps.

He asked me what record, and I told him that in Korea in 1950, I was a Staff Sergeant and fifty years later, I had been promoted to Gunney Sergeant. "Fifty years between promotions—I believe that's a record for the Marines."

He laughed and said, "That's not only a record for the Marine Corps—but for all the services."

I was just joking with him. It was a wonderful rewarding event in Washington and I felt very humbled by the recognition of the Silver Star Award.

An article appeared in the September, 2000, edition of The Marine's magazine, "The Leatherneck", chronicling the events of that Korean War event. It was titled "Chosin Heroism Rewarded". In the article Colonel Alpha Browser, Operations officer of the First Marine Division during the Korean War, called the defense of Fox Company "an epic of courage... to go down beside the proudest and most honored deeds of our nation's wars."

In the "Stars and Stripes" issue, July 13-16, Shelley Davis wrote an article entitled "After the War, A Star of Redemption. It states that the medal was supposed to be awarded at the end of the War. "Somehow the paper work got lost in the fog of war." With me, I didn't mind at all. It was good—fifty years later—to experience the honor of having the Commandant himself pin the star on me and have the feeling of redemption that came with it.

In the Marine Corps Museum in Triangle, Virginia, just outside Washington, D.C., an entire room is dedicated to the memory of those who fought in what is referred to as "the forgotten war". The words describing the exhibit are:

"On Toktong Pass in the Chosin Reservoir visitors may encounter Marines who are cold, tired, and short of ammunition. It's after midnight with the light of a full moon behind them. Visitors feel the cold; they hear the Chinese soldiers advancing up the snowy mountain, and watch while the Marines, bundled against the December weather, prepare for the next attack. They are quietly resolved to win." Marines know no other way to do their job except by "resolving to win"! And then doing it!

Billy and Dot leaving for Washington for Silver Star Presentation

Billy receiving Silver Star From US Commandant Jimmy Jones

Silver Star Medal

Newspaper clipping of Billy receiving Silver Star

Billy at Marine Corps Museum in Washington

Billy and Sergeant Major John Henry (who led Billy's platoon and saved his life on one or more times.)

"He will yet fill your mouth with laughter and your lips with shouts of joy,"

Job 8: 21 niv

CHAPTER 20

BACK TO KOREA

THREE YEARS AFTER I was awarded the Silver Star, I received an invitation to go back to Korea. It was 2003 and the South Korean government was having a 50 year commemoration of the end of the Korean War. A special presentation was being held to assure those who served in the war that "A Grateful Nation Remembers" and appreciates the sacrifices made on their behalf. The conflict had begun on June 25, 1950, when the North Korean People's Army had invaded South Korea. It had officially ended on November 11, 1953.

All expenses for the trip were to be paid by the Korean government. It was an honor to fly out to Los Angeles to meet the 53 other veterans of the Korean War for the 14 hour flight to the South Korean International Airport outside of Inchon, South Korea. I had been with the First Marine Division which made the Inchon Landing in 1950 to cut the North Korean army off and begin to retake the country.

From the airport we were bused to our hotel in Seoul, Korea's capital city. Along the way it was exciting to see that the scars and devastation of war had virtually disappeared.

The World Cup had just been held there. Flags were still flying. We could see the stadium where this important athletic event had been held.

Our days were spent touring South Korea. What a difference to see Seoul now instead of from the viewpoint of a Marine fighting to drive an invading army out. When we had left Seoul in 1950, the city was pretty much in ashes and bombed out buildings.

One of the highlights of the week was going to the site where the North Korean government came together with the United States and South Korea to confirm the end of the Korean War. I stood in awe at the DMZ—the demilitarized zone which separates North Korea from South Korea where I could see the North Korean soldiers patrolling their side of their border—only a few feet away from us.

Even though there are United States service men still on duty in Korea, it is a free country with a democratic government and a thriving way of life for its people.

When we Marines left in 1950, we were pushing North Korean soldiers back across the 38th parallel, retaking territory they had secured when they invaded the country. It was a war-torn place, burning from the bombs and napalm dropped by Corsair pilots. Now, 50 years later, it was a beautiful city, a nation rebuilt, a state of the art city with massive skyscrapers—apartments and office buildings—one of the most beautiful, clean, crime free, inviting cities one could ever visit.

The city was alive with millions of people going about their business—and their pleasure.

Some of the people were patronizing American fast food shops such as Baskin-Robbins and I had lunch at a McDonald's with one of our Southern Baptist missionaries who had been in the country for fourteen years. He told me that South Korea was now sending missionaries to the United States. He spoke of the safety of living there, the low incidence of crime, pointed out the great number of mopeds people rode that were parked on the streets with no locks needed on them. The city was clean. A state of the art underground transportation system was in operation I visited the University of Soeul, learned that children start to school very early and go long days there. Education is at a premium.

It was easy to see that South Koreans are hardworking people—industrious, creative, proud of their freedom and willing to take advantage of all that freedom offers.

WHILE THERE, I had the privilege of attending the largest Christian church in the world which has a membership of more than a million people. Having gone to church all of my life, it was a pleasure to see and be a part of a worship service in the most dynamic church I could ever hope to experience. Their freedom, as does ours, guarantees them also the right to worship as they choose.

A banquet was held for us on our final night there. Many officials expressed appreciation and presented us with commemorative medals.

AS WE WERE flying out of Korea on our way home, my thoughts were full of questions: What was it we had been fighting for there? What was it that many of my fellow Marines—friends—had given their lives there for? The conflict was, after all, considered a stalemate. The theme of the celebration was: "Freedom Is Not Free". How well I knew that, for I had been there when hundreds of my peers had given their lives to secure it for them. Many spending the rest of the lives they had handicapped or crippled. Had it been worth it all or was it just a waste of time and precious life?

And it came to me in vivid assurance that these people were now living in a democratic society—in freedom—not the oppression of communism as North Korea is and would have imposed on their South Korean neighbors had they been allowed to succeed in their attempt to overtake them. I knew then—and now know-without a doubt, seeing what I had witnessed in the past few days, what the country had become, how they have prospered, what a good lifestyle the people have—that our efforts, our sacrifice—it was all worthwhile!

Billy on trip back to Korea overlooking DMZ

Billy in Back to Korea celebration in front of McDonald's

"You realize, don't you, that you are the temple of God, and God himself is present in you? No one will get by with vandalizing God's temple. You can be sure of that. God's temple is sacred—and you, remember, are the temple."

I Corinthians 3: 16 msg

CHAPTER 21

HALE AND HEARTY

ONE OF THE outstanding blessings I've had in my life is that of good health. Missing school because of illness wasn't something I had to contend with except for those first grade encounters with measles, chicken pox and mumps. I breezed through the remainder of my school experience, my Marine Corps days, and rarely missed a day of work for any physical ailment—certainly not for health reasons. The good food my Mother fed me, the exercise and fresh outdoor air that was imposed on me with the farm work and the regimen of running, walking, and exercising that I had maintained throughout my life really paid off.

I was a healthy, hardy, hale specimen of humanity!

It was a big shock to me when, in 1989 I began to experience pain in my abdomen, pain so severe that it sometimes caused me to double up and fall to the floor. I began to have to get up several times a night for trips to the bathroom. It was disruptive and disabling. The football coach at Hendersonville High School where I was director of the counseling program recognized the symptoms from having been there himself and suggested I see his doctor, Dr. Nesbitt, who had treated him successfully. I did!

It took only a brief examination and tests for him to determine that I needed surgery and that as soon as possible. I was more than ready to follow his advice.

The morning after the surgery, Dr. Nesbitt came

into my room and said: "Mr. DeVasher, you are the luckiest man alive today. There was a small cancer and we were able to remove it. That was 25 years ago and there's been no reoccurrence of that problem.

However, fifteen years later, I had to visit a dermatologist—having had frequent exposure to the sun throughout my life—to ask about a growth on my face. The growth was fine, but he found a spot on my leg—hardly larger than a pin point—a blue mole looking innocent enough to me. I said to him, "It's just a little mole".

He replied: "We need to send it to the lab for testing."

I was kidding, "With a little mole like that, you'll probably have to cut my leg off."

He didn't think it too humorous. About a week later there was a call from his office. The test had revealed that the mole in fact was Melanoma—level four—with level five being the most serious.

I was amazed at the speed with which they referred me to a specialist who scheduled me for surgery at the Vanderbilt Hospital to remove a significant amount of the muscle in my leg and lymph nodes for that part of my body.

My reaction to this was unusual—for me! I just put the whole thing in God's hands and was very calm and nonchalant about the whole business.

The same report came back from him that I had gotten from Dr. Nesibtt—"We got the cancer and the lymph nodes were clear." However, I go for check-ups every 4 months and they keep a careful lookout for this disease that likes to hide in a person's body and do its destructive work in a secret way until it's too late for treatment to be effective. So far, so good, thank God! No reoccurrence!

That was then. This is now.

I never realized that life could be so easy now that I've passed my 85th year of life. I have time to go to the gym three or four times a week to work out, which I have been doing for the past 3or 4 years. It's become a lifestyle I maintain even though I have a few health issues:

The damage to my feet from being frozen in Korea.

Knees worn out from running since the early 1970's—

I was running 10 miles a day when my knees gave out. Surgery ended the running. Now I walk several times a week. I met a friend one day while walking who had been a runner. He was walking too. He had to quit playing pro-football because of his knees. I asked him how his walking was compared to running. His reply: "It's like kissing your sister." That pretty well describes it.

But I keep on walking and working out! Not just for pleasure, although it makes me feel good. Maybe it will result in longevity of life.

Three orthopedic surgeons have examined my feet—X-rays, Cat scans, MRI's. They all tell me the same thing. The nerves in my feet are damaged from being frozen at the Chosin Reservoir on Fox Hill in North Korea. In addition to nerve damage, arthritis has set in. Surgery is too complicated. I asked the doctor: What do I do then? He said: "Walk through the pain, but keep walking. If you stop, you will lose your ability to walk at all."

So I walk! If exercising and eating right will enable me to live better and longer, then I'm all for it.

I RECENTLY HEARD someone say: "Every day I have is a gift from God. He gives me this gift—that's why each day is called the present." Each day! A present from the Lord of the Universe.

I have lived to bury all of my immediate family and most of my wife's family. My wife and I have talked on several occasions in recent years and decided that we aren't going to focus on our ailments and waste our time complaining. In the time we have left here on earth, we will simply recognize how blessed we are and give thanks for those blessings!

I knew when I came off Fox Hill with the handful of Marines who survived—that everything from that point on would be downhill—all the way. And it has been!

I met a man named Paul the other day at the gym where I work out. He comes walking with a cane and goes from one workout station to another on that cane. He is a retired medical doctor who moved here from California to care for his daughter who is ill. He is 90 years old. I said; "That's amazing Paul. You have me beat. I'm only 85." He said, "Not so amazing. I have an older brother who is 107." When

I asked him how he felt about being 90, he replied, "I don't know. It came so soon."

My life has been good. I didn't realize how good until I attended my high school reunion and found there are only three men left who played on the football squad. I told one of the players that we were going to be the last ones standing. Now he has passed away.

It's then that you face your mortality. The Bible says that we (that includes me) are made by Him, in His image, and that each of us is an original—a special person. Nobody like me! Or you! Unique! It also says that "in Him we live and move and have our being." It's all in His hands! Wherever He takes me, the best is yet to come. He has made a way for me in this world and in the world to come—where I will meet Him, the Lord of Lords and the King of Kings who is the source of all that has happened to me in this life.

The apostle Paul wrote in his second letter to the Corinthians (2: 9)

"Eye has not seen, ear has not heard, neither has entered into the heart of man, the things that God has prepared for those who love Him."

His letter to Timothy (II Timothy 4: 7) is the goal worthy for reaching for:

"I have fought the good fight, I have finished the race; I have kept the faith. Finally there is laid up for me a crown of righteousness which the Lord, the righteous Judge, will give to me on that day, and not to me only but also to all who have loved Him."

The finish line is just ahead! I have no illusions about my worthiness to cross it. I know, better than most, that I am a sinner!

But I also know—beyond a shadow or a doubt that when the Man from Nazareth, the Son of God, was handing on that cross, that He was there in my place, paying the price for my sins, securing my place in eternity with Him! And He has a place for everybody else who is willing to believe Him—regardless of who you are, what you have done, where you are from, or what credentials you may possess! The only requirement? Accepting the gift of what He's done for you!

Billy in the Fall of 2012 visiting U.S Marine Corps Museum in Triangle, Virginia

"I have fought the good fight. I have finished the race, I have kept the faith. Finally, there is laid up for me a crown of righteousness, which the Lord, the righteous Judge, will give to me on that day, and not to me only but to all who have loved His appearing!

         II Timothy 4: 7-8 nlt

CHAPTER 22

85 AND HOLDING

HAPPY BIRTHDAY, DOKES! My family calls me "Dokes". Dokes is the name given to me by my first grandchild, Ryan. We aren't sure where he got it. We only know that it stuck and all the children, children-in-law and grandchildren now call me "Dokes". And now that two great grandchildren are on the scene, I'm sure they'll join the others.

It is January 18, 2013. It is my 85th birthday! The tradition in our family is that the whole clan gets together at some point (usually a Sunday) to celebrate birthdays—and mine was today.!

The "Happy Birthday, Dokes" phrase had rung out all afternoon from all directions, from everybody.

The "Happy Birthday" song has been sung. The gifts opened. The cake and ice cream devoured!

The party is over! The gang has retired to their separate vehicles, backed out of the driveway and driven away!

And HERE I AM! I breathe a sigh of relief and collapse into my favorite chair in the sunroom. The lights are out and I light a candle! It is time to take stock of all this, to do a little serious thinking—meditating, if you please. Maybe it will help me get a handle on what I'm experiencing right now inside of me, of what I'm feeling!

That feeling? A deep sense of contentment! Contentment? Not a sensation that's been a frequent companion of mine over the years,. In fact, the exact opposite more nearly describes my stance—the "let's get on with it" attitude—there's more out there and we have to get it—today—right now! Let's get going!

But NOW, I've settled into the warm, comfortable coziness of seeing LIFE as it really is, of discovering the Truth of what it's all about. Allow me to share some of what I've learned....

My first discovery about life is: how short it is. In terms of life expectancy, we think living eighty-five years is beating the system! And actually, I've lived long enough to bury all the members of my birth family and many of my friends, but I look back and wonder how I got here so fast! Where did it all go?

It shouldn't be any surprise, however. We've been warned about that in the wisest book ever written—the Bible. The Psalmist said in Psalm 39:4-5:

"Lord, make me to know my end, and what is the measure of my days, that I may know how frail I am, Indeed, You have made my days as handbreadths,

And my age is as nothing before You, Certainly every man at his best state is but a vapor."

And the book of James (4: 14) in the New Testament affirms that thought:

"…For what is your life? It is even a vapor that appears for a little time and then vanishes away."

And so, it is no surprise that I'm nearing the finish line of my life here on earth!

With few, with no regrets!

For life has been like a school for me!

I can agree with the Apostle Paul who said of his life: "I know how to be abased, and I know how to abound. Everywhere and in all things, I have learned both to be full and to be hungry, both to abound and to suffer need." (Philippians 4: 12)

Need I remind you of my ups and downs:

I have been young and I am now old by the world's standards.

I have lived with a definite void of education (even failing first Grade) and have received four graduate degrees—including a doctorate in Theology.

I have lived through both multiple failures and multiple successes.

I have been broke living on $37.50 a week and having the tires on my car facing repossession, and I have at one point accumulated $1,000,000 dollars.

I have lived alone and I have had the blessing of life with my wife for 60 years—and a healthy, thriving family.

I have listened as a doctor speaks the word, cancer, to me, and I have enjoyed good health and a great, active life physically.

And I have had the blessing of being able to identify with people in many walks of life—because I have been there:

I ran a paper route.

I sold ice—big blocks of ice—door to door—in the days when people still had only ice boxes;

I was a buyer for a strawberry processing company working with farmers who grew strawberries.

I operated a bulldozer.

I farmed for a while raising cattle and pigs.

I worked in the Caterpillar Tractor Factory as an on-the-liner.

I experienced the wheat harvest in Oklahoma from before dawn to after dusk.

I baked bread for the Colonial Bread Company

I was an X-"Ray Technician with the Tennessee Mobile Unit.

I was a specialty salesman—knocking on doors to sell encyclopedias, food plans, cemetery lots.

I was a machine gunner with the U.S Marine Corps in World War II and the Korean War.

I was owner-operator of several Health Spas.

I have been a Real Estate Broker,

Real Estate Developer

Builder of both single family and multiple family dwellings,

I was a commodity trader with the Chicago Board of Trade

I have for 55 years been a preacher, minister, pastor of Baptist churches in several states

I have taught school

Coached high school athletic teams.

I have served as a counselor of both high school students and for patients in drug facilities.

I know the struggles that go with living in all walks of life, because I have been there.

Tonight as I reminisce about all this, I arrive at one very definite, very real conclusion: The reality that GOD IS and that He is wants to be involved on a daily, very personal basis in the life of anyone who is willing to turn to Him and turn that place of involvement over to Him.

I'm persuaded that the foundation of a life well-lived has to be based on the truth that God IS. He said it over and over through the centuries—I AM! On the heels of living eight and a half decades with all its ups and downs, I know beyond a shadow of a doubt that God is in his Heaven and that He is Creator, Savior, Shepherd, and King of Kings to whoever will believe Him and trust Him.

I believe Him. I have trusted Him. He has walked with me all the way—even when I did not know He was there.

And He had guided me with a love that is completely unconditional—never being dependent on what I did or did not do—just on the fact that His beloved Son paid the price it took to forgive my sins and buy me out of the muddle of my own doing and lead me into the Kingdom of His love.

I know that when He said: He would guide me with His eye (Psalm 32: 8)—the eye that sees the past, present, and future—that I was in good hands.

There is no way that I could have lived this story if God had not been directing my life—unbeknown to me. A friend of mine recently looked me straight in the eye and said, DeVasher, you have had an angel assigned just to you!"

This book isn't about me; it can't be about me. It's about God and how he moved in my life. The Bible says that "we live and love and have our being in Him" (Acts 17: 28). I know for a fact that is true.

There's no way I could have ever gotten off Fox Hill—out of the trap with the odds greatly against that happening—by myself. It had to be His provision. There would be no way to survive by will and skill alone.

There's no way I could have ever earned four degrees from prodigious colleges, universities, and seminaries on my own. The odds were just as great as they were on Fox Hill—maybe even greater. I had bombed out miserably in three colleges. The odds were overwhelming. It all happened because of God's supernatural involvement.

There's no way the odds of my marrying my high school girl friend after the passing of eight years from our first date until we stood at the altar in the same little town where we grew up—the greatest odds of all against that happening. Little did we know at the time that this marriage had been made in Heaven. Again—overwhelming odds! God must have had a hand in it all!

But God doesn't pay any attention to odds!

Or we would never have heard the account of David and Goliath's encounter!

Who would have thought we would celebrate a 60th wedding anniversary? Who would have envisioned a family of three children, the three children-in-laws that they married, six grandchildren, and two great grandchildren at this date—with the three children still married to the same spouses—as well as two grandchildren married?

Nobody! It's all because of the grace and mercy of a loving Heavenly Father who so loved us all that "He gave His only begotten Son that whosoever believes in Him shall not perish from the earth but have life everlasting." (John 3: 16) It's all because that Son, Jesus gave himself saying "I have come that they may have live and that more abundantly." (John 10: 10)

My story is "To God be the glory" for what He has done. I am assured He will continue to do. John said in his writing (John 1: 14) "We have seen His glory, the glory of the One and only, who came from the Father, full of grace and mercy." The theme of my story, my new song is: To Him be the glory for his grace and mercy to me!

The DeVasher family at wedding of granddaughter, A.J. and Brian Melton—before grandchild, Ella Jane Melton was born. Billy performed the ceremony.

DeVasher family on vacation
at Rosemary Beach, Fla—2012
(Missing: Jeff Kolb, Maddie Kolb, Brian Melton)

Billy and Dot at 50th Wedding Anniversary celebration

"I have not achieved it, but I focus on this one thing: forgetting the past and looking forward to what is ahead, I press on to reach the end of the race and receive the heavenly prize for which God, through Christ Jesus, is calling us."

Philippians 3: 13-14 nlt

EPILOGUE

So—that's my story!

So far!

It isn't over yet!

There's more to come!

I was praying the other day—really I was just talking to God and I told him I wanted to take on another project. It was something I felt like I could do, but there was one thing holding me back, so I said to the Lord:

"I want to do this, Lord, and I think I can do it, but I'm 85 years old, and …"

And the Lord interrupted me:"

"So what?" he said.

I stopped short, shook my head a little bit and continued: "Lord, I believe I misunderstood you. Did you say So What?"

"So what if you're 85 in earth years?"

The answer was clear. (I have this habit of talking to the Lord—but never really listening. It was impossible to mistake his reply this time.)

"Yes, I said: SO WHAT? You're still breathing, aren't you? You are still ambulatory, aren't you? You really aren't finished in this world until I say you are, are you? So keep on keeping on, doing the work I tell you to do, living! I'll come for you when the time is right. I AM your shepherd, the good shepherd. Keep your eyes on me and follow along…"

Remember—My "eye is on the sparrow and I know He's watching me."

That's what I intend to do—from here on into eternity! Just keep my eye on the One who always has His eye on me!

ABOUT THE AUTHOR

Having read the book this far, you probably have a pretty good picture of its author. It's one of a man who faced incredible odds, difficult circumstances, difficult obstacles and was delivered from them all by the power and presence of a living Lord in his life. It is his intention to give all the praise and glory for the victories won.

Now that he has passed his 85th birthday, he enjoys a full, active, productive living with his wife of 60 plus years in Hendersonville, Tennessee. He is blessed by his family of three children and their spouses, six grandchildren (two of whom are married), and two great grandchildren. Billy is a member of the First Baptist Church in Hendersonville, Tennessee and also a lifetime member of Disabled American Veterans, American Legion, and Veterans of Foreign Wars.

He would be further blessed by hearing your reaction to his story.

He can be reached by:

    E-mail: billydevasher@comcast.net

    Mail at: 131 Forest Retreat Road
                Hendersonville, TN 37075

    Phone: 615-824-7077

    Cell: 615-679-5224